To Rosie & Bill

Don't take any!

Bon Voyage

Alan

Wooden Nickels

WOODEN NICKELS

Or, the Decline and Fall
of Silver Coins

William F. Rickenbacker

ARLINGTON HOUSE

New Rochelle, New York

To E.V.R.
FATHER, FRIEND, ADVISOR

with the hope
that the sound money you
grew up with
will circulate once again
in the days of your grandchildren

When and if the day of silver's 'depoliticalization' comes, whether it be *de facto* or *de jure,* it will be a day of triumph for those lonely thinkers who have insisted all along that the free market can be counted on eventually to solve everything. On that day the shades of William Jennings Bryan and a whole host of his Free Silverite and Populist followers will spin rapidly in their graves. But what they fought for—a 'just' price for silver—would be a reality all the more welcome because it represented a natural evolution of the law of supply and demand.

—JOHN CHAMBERLAIN
Barron's, April 4, 1955

Contents

Preface 9

1. The Great Coin Shortage 13

2. Silver: Supply and Demand 33

3. Silver and the U.S. Treasury 53

4. The Treasury Muffs the Challenge 72

5. Problems in Altering a Coinage 97

6. President Johnson Flunks Out 113

7. An Opportunity Missed 133

8. The Outlook 145

Notes 159

Glossary 164

Appendix: Extracts from
   *Treasury Staff Study of
   Silver and Coinage* 169

Preface

AROUND YEAR-END 1965, the United States entered a new period in its monetary history. Future writers will call it the flight from silver, the abandonment of silver, the liberation from silver—depending on their own attitudes. No matter what they call it, they will no doubt agree that the event was one of peculiar importance. A silver coinage practically unchanged from the birth of the republic went out of circulation and was replaced by a coinage of base metal.

This monetary event was unusual in another way, too. It was visible, indeed in one sense it was tangible. Most monetary happenings have a way of being carried out in the bowels of central banks and are of interest only to professional observers. A shift in the rate for federal funds, a new way to treat vault cash, a change in the gold reserve clause—these events may carry much more serious meaning for each citizen, but they are largely unheard and unseen. Not so with a revolution in the coinage. Every citizen over the age of seven or eight will see and feel the new coinage, compare it with the old, perhaps think about it, and surely at some point make up his mind whether it is preferable to spend the new or the old coin.

Because the matter is important and because it is of general interest, I have thought to write this short book explaining the origin of the silver crisis, the kind of problems it posed for the Federal Government, the response of Washington, and the prospects for the new coinage. This is done in terms that are readily understandable to the general reader—inescapably so, because I am no expert in monetary matters myself, and am writing only from the standpoint of general interest and close observation over a period of three or four years.

It is my duty in the interest of fairness to mention that I am no expert, but at the same time I would dissuade the reader from making a federal case out of it. The higher complexities of modern monetary systems may very well be the private demesnes of only the rarest spirits, but coinage is something else again. Of all the forms of money that we use these days, coinage is the oldest. Men have had coins jingling in their hands for about 4,600 years. Our youngsters begin using coins in real transactions at an early age, and the institutional framework of modern American life *requires* the young to start using coins as soon as they start going to school and buying their own lunch. Very early we begin to wonder about the peculiar power of a round bit of metal, that a grown man should be willing to accept it in return for "giving" a real ice cream cone to a young boy. After a few years have gone by, the average citizen understands a good deal about the peculiar power of those bits of metal. They change hands because "everyone knows they're okay" (conventional sanction), because "they're worth something" (intrinsic value), because the government requires them to be accepted in payment of debt (legal tender), because they stand for work previously done (the boy earns a coin cutting grass, the grocer earns the boy's coin making ice cream available), and for other similar reasons, none of which is beyond the comprehension of any serious adult.

It is a pleasure to recall the many people who have been of great help in the preparation of this work, whether they knew it or not. My original interest in the silver problem must be traced back to a casual conversation with my former colleague, the brilliant Mr. D. G. M. Coxe of Toronto, whose mastery of the problem more than four years ago inspired me to emulate his adeptness. I have enjoyed the great privilege of informal conversations on the matter with the amiable and peerless Prof. Milton Friedman and with the profound and courtly Henry Hazlitt, neither of whom should be tarred with the brush of my conclusions, which are of course exclusively my responsibility. My large-hearted employer and admirable friend William F. Buckley Jr. agreed to make time available to me for work on projects such as this; it is a pleasure to mention this as only a sample of his uncounted beneficences over the years.

I record here also my thanks to Dr. Elgin Groseclose for permission to quote the lengthy passage from his fine work, *Money and Man,* and to D. Van Nostrand for permission to quote the great narrative paragraph from the late Benjamin Anderson's incomparable *Economics and the Public Welfare.* The Foundation for Economic Education has generously allowed me the run of its magnificent library.

To my lovely wife Alexandra for maintaining order in the household whilst I tried to write, and to James and Thomas for consenting, in their fashion, to the maintenance of said order, I owe much much more than can be expressed in these few words.

W. F. R.

Briarcliff Manor, New York
November 1, 1965

1. The Great Coin Shortage

THE UNITED STATES is in the final stage of a long-term monetary experience which will culminate, all too probably, in the disappearance of silver coin from circulation. There is every indication that the United States Government was taken by surprise, although the first of a long series of warning signals was visible ten years ago. A separate chapter is devoted to the lethargic and uncomprehending career of the Treasury during the decade when the signs were multiplying that this nation was heading for its deepest monetary embarrassment since the stock market crash of 1929. At the outset I want to give some idea of the size and shape of the problem, and of the various responses that have been offered or may be offered.

The banking system first felt a pinch on coins in 1962. The Federal Reserve Bank of New York received from general circulation slightly less small change than it had received in 1961. As with almost every monetary experience, there has been not only an acceleration towards the end, but an acceleration in the rate of acceleration. In 1963 the New York Federal Reserve Bank received 20 per cent less small change from general circulation than it had in 1962. In 1964 it received 63 per cent less than in 1963. "For the second consecutive year," reported Mr. Alfred Hayes, President of the Federal Reserve Bank of New York, "the shortage of coins necessitated a general rationing of shipments to banks. At various times during 1964, such shipments were reduced to a token one or two bags of certain denominations and had to be suspended completely on several occasions."[1]

By the middle of 1964 a "grey market" had developed for small coin. An officer of a Cleveland bank admitted that he was sometimes paying $2 extra for a bag of $200 in nickels. A peanut and candy machine vendor reported he was doing a "brisk" business selling $25 worth of pennies for $28; and $50 worth of nickels, dimes, and quarters for $55. According to Del E. Webb Corp., which operates two hotels and a casino in Las Vegas through a subsidiary, large lots of coins ($1,000 worth) were trading at a 20 per cent premium. The vice president of a bank in Chicago reported that he had lost several good sources of coins: local churches. Independent coin wholesalers were offering such fat premiums for the church collections that the churches had no choice but to turn away from the banks. The Horn & Hardart cafeteria chain reported that it was often down to a two-hour supply of coins; in the past it had always kept about a week's supply on hand. The Federal Reserve Bank of Atlanta reported early in June that it had $200,000 in coins on hand—down from $3.5 million, five years earlier. The comptroller of a New York City store chain reported that if he asked the bank for $25 in change he'd be given $3. Banks began appealing to the public to bring in their small change. A bank in Orlando offered a $1 bill for every 98 cents in coin. A bank in Atlanta offered a free lunch to any employee who turned in $100 in pennies. A midwestern grocery chain got wind of a 3½-ton pile of U.S. pennies in a Canadian bank; it sent a top executive to negotiate the deal, and gladly footed the bill for transporting the coins back to their home country. A bank in San Francisco, when coin shipments from Colorado dried up, began trucking in nickels from Oregon at its own expense. The Philadelphia Mint shipped $30,000 in nickels to Las Vegas; one week later Las Vegas reported a nickel shortage. Casino managements were emptying the slot machines every four hours in order to keep their customers supplied with coin.[2]

In Boston, by mid-1964, the managers of supermarkets were scurrying from laundromats to machine vendors to church elders in a frantic effort to get some coin. Bank employees in Atlanta were quietly slipping bags of coins to coin dealers for a 10 per cent premium. A California bank launched an advertising campaign to persuade the children to empty their piggy banks. The Jewel Tea Company announced that it would print multi-colored scrip for its Chicago area stores, in denominations of one cent, five cents, and ten cents; the Treasury frowned, said something about prosecution for counterfeiting, and persuaded Jewel Tea to drop the idea. In Monroe, Wisconsin, the First National Bank spent $400 of its own hard-earned money to manufacture 20,000 wooden nickels, which the local merchants had agreed to accept in circulation. Before the Treasury could impound these most legendary of counterfeits, the good citizens of Monroe had swept up all but 450 of them. As keepsakes, of course.[3]

The Kroger Company had selected a design for its scrip, and National Tea and First National Stores were seriously considering issuing scrip themselves, when the Treasury's unamused response to the Jewel Tea scrip put an end to their plans.[2]

New York bus drivers and taxi drivers who turned in their coins at Nedick's snack bars would, more often than not, get a free cup of coffee for their pains. The S. H. Kress Company had to fly $5,000 in coin from Baltimore to New York to meet a serious local shortage. New York banks serving predominantly retail store areas were turning down many of their customers' requests for coin. Said one banker, "It is terribly embarrassing." In New York, as in Boston, the executives of retail store chains were approaching the elders of the churches with attractive terms for the Sunday collections. The main office of the First National City Bank had only $300 in pennies—to meet the needs of the bank's 126 local branch offices. A friend at the Chase Manhattan said, "We got only $6,900 in coin from the Federal Reserve Bank of New York, where only recently we were drawing from $600,000 to $700,000 a week." The head teller of the Marine Midland Trust Company was informed that the Federal Reserve couldn't give him any coins for the next three weeks. The New York Federal Reserve Bank reported that it had $600,000 in coins on hand, whereas "for efficient operation we need $6 million to $7 million." The Great Atlantic and Pacific Tea Company posted signs at each checkout counter, asking the customers to offer the exact change if possible; and with good results. Loew's and RKO movie houses were raiding their own concession stands for small change, and even in some instances scrounging some coins from local storekeepers.[4]

"We are experiencing a critical coin shortage," said Mr. William McChesney Martin, Chairman of the Board of Governors of the Federal Reserve System, on July 1, 1964. "As commercial banks have found themselves with less and less excess coin, the return flow to the Reserve Banks has dwindled. Deliveries of new coin from the mint have risen, but this added supply has been more than offset by the drying

up of return flows of coin from circulation. Today...the return flow has shrunk to the point where it is now less than
the amount of new coin received from the mint; in more
normal times, the return flow was nine times as great as
receipts from the mint. In consequence, inventories have
fallen to the point where the Reserve Banks have been unable to deliver coins on request, but instead have been forced
to ration coins in order to distribute the limited supply on a
fair basis."[5]

Mr. Lawrence A. Rubin, President of the American Bridge,
Tunnel, and Turnpike Association, and Executive Secretary
of the Mackinac Bridge Authority (Michigan), reported that
toll collectors were feeling the pinch in coins. The managers
of the New Jersey Turnpike tried to ease the situation by making a "Monday morning collection" among churches along
the turnpike. Around Pittsburgh the Pennsylvania Turnpike
people were trying to get their hands on small coin by collecting the coin from the Turnpike concessionaire, Howard
Johnson Inc.[6] A Nantucket merchant minted his own coins,
bearing the whale emblem of his island, redeemable until
1970. They circulated good as gold until the Treasury re-
minded him of the laws about counterfeiting.[7]

In Kansas City, Missouri, the City National Bank & Trust
Company was offering a 1 per cent premium for coins turned
in during a certain three-week period. The person turning in
the largest amount of coin got his choice of a two-week vacation for two in Florida or a check for $1,000. Second prize
was a one-week vacation at Lake of the Ozarks, or $500 in
cash. The next three winners received savings accounts of
$100, $50, and $25.[8]

"I've got it!" cries the shaggy bird perched on the shell of a
land turtle, in Mr. John Hart's cartoon series, "B.C." It is

November 16, 1964. "I've got the answer to the coin short-age!" continues the bird. The turtle, ever the straight man, asks, "What is it?" Shaggy bird says, triumphantly, "Raise the price of everything to a buck."[9]

Shortly before Christmas of 1964 a major newspaper ran a long article on the problem of the disappearing coinage, reproducing the advertisements that had been distributed by various business organizations. There was the old-fashioned "Wanted—Your extra coins, to help us stem the current COIN SHORTAGE—please help us by bringing in any extra coins you may have—The Chase Manhattan Bank." And there was "Nation-Wide COIN SHORTAGE—Do you have the exact change for your purchase?—If so, we will appreciate your help—Thank you—A & P Food Stores." And "During the Coin Shortage—We have been having an awful time trying to get together enough coins to make change. We would greatly appreciate it...." etc., signed, Chock Full o' Nuts.[10]

A strange thing happened on January 13, 1965. An American firm paid good money to advertise the virtues of a foreign coinage. "This coin," said the spacious advertisement in the newspapers, "has been in circulation in Switzerland for 80 years." The picture shows the coin held between anonymous thumb and forefinger, and in the background there looms the usual Matterhorn. The coin looks fresh and shiny. "How can it look so good?" asks Madison Avenue. The answer is immediate: "It's made of nickel." The advertisement was published by International Nickel Company.[11]

Also in January 1965 the Chase Manhattan Bank sent to each of its clients a notice that said: "The simple nickel (and dime, penny, quarter, half) are in temporary short supply. They'll never be extinct, but there just aren't enough coins in circulation these days. We at Chase Manhattan need more coins. . . . So what can you do? Break that piggy bank. Empty that drawer. Open that fat jar of pennies. And bring your coins into the Bank. . . . We'll then swap you even for crisp new bills (we've got plenty of them). Sound fair?" The irony was not lost on everyone. There were some who remembered how the first John Rockefeller had spent his twilight years giving away dimes with silver in them, and who smiled to learn that Mr. John Rockefeller's grandson at the Chase Manhattan was convinced that it was almost a patriotic obligation to turn in one's dimes and get "crisp new bills" in exchange.

At the very moment when the Chase Manhattan was asserting that the present U.S. coins would "never be extinct," another bank was acting more objectively. The January 1965 issue of the *Central Economic Letter,* a monthly newsletter of the Central National Bank of Cleveland, carried an article by Dr. Clain-Stefanelli, Curator of Numismatics of the U.S. National Museum. Dr. Clain-Stefanelli wrote: "The critical decision which must be made promptly is to abandon silver coinage in an orderly manner, while the silver problem is still subject to control. Undeniably, silver coinage has served the world well. But now the time has come, after more than 2,500 years, to set sentiment aside and to close out the career of silver, recognizing that the commercial needs of modern society with its vast industrial appetites and its exploding population, can no longer be met in the old way."[12]

And, despite enormous efforts to increase the coinage, the Federal Reserve had to report in February 1965 that there was still a noticeable shortage of dimes, quarters, and half dollars.[13] Those who are interested in the art of writing headlines may be amused to know that the story that carried this information was published under the headline: "Mint Begins to Make Dent In Nation's Coin Shortage." The last sentence of the article reported that the Federal Reserve holdings of subsidiary silver coinage were *lower* than they had been a year earlier.

The evidence is conclusive. Beginning in 1961, the U.S. coinage gradually seeped out of the banking system. A coin shortage was felt, and reported, throughout the nation. Three coins had almost completely disappeared from circulation by the end of 1965: the silver dollar, the 1964 Kennedy half dollar, and the wartime nickel of the 1940s. Of the remaining types of coins there seemed to be enough to do business in a limping sort of way, but the banks were on short rations and were in turn passing out short rations, the situation was obviously abnormal, and there were no signs of improvement.

But this did not exist in a vacuum. People were making the decision to hold coin rather than other forms of money. Who were these people?

In March 1964 that question arose in a startling way. Crowds of people descended upon the Treasury building in Washington to demand silver dollars. They carried their coins away in little red wagons, brief cases, flight bags, and Army surplus ammunition boxes. "This damned nonsense of coin collecting," said one Treasury official.[14] The story had spread that the Treasury was dipping into its hoard of "Morgan" dollars (named after the designer, and minted before World War I), some of which are greatly fancied by collectors. Treasury officials noted that many of the collectors would pick over their coins and bring the unwanted silver dollars back to the Treasury. In an attempt to shrug off such folly, the Treasury pointedly mentioned that it was largely passing out last week's rejects.

And so for the first time the theory achieved prominence that the coin shortage was to be traced to coin collectors. Unfortunately, the theory broke down at the start. If the Treasury officials were right, then all the silver dollars without numismatic value would be returned to the Treasury. They were not returned. On Wednesday, March 25, 1964, the Treasury announced that it would no longer pay out silver dollars. Of the 485 million silver dollars supposed to exist, only 3 million remained in the Treasury. The Treasury did not know how to distribute those 3 million fairly amongst all the claimants. So it locked them up. The characteristic acceleration towards the end of a monetary trend is present in the decline of the Treasury's holdings of silver dollars:

YEAR-END	Treasury Stock of Silver Dollars (millions)
1954	267.6
1955	253.5
1956	236.3
1957	219.0
1958	202.7
1959	182.3
1960	161.2
1961	130.1
1962	94.0
1963	28.5
(March 1964)	2.9

I shall return to the great question of the silver dollar, and the reasons for its disappearance, in a later chapter. At the moment, this weird episode at the Treasury is relevant because it provided the shock that was necessary, apparently, to open people's eyes to the much larger problem of the coin shortage in general. The Treasury had asked for funds to mint a batch of silver dollars. The House Appropriations Committee rejected the idea, insisting that the real problem was elsewhere. "The shortage in minor coins," said the Committee report, "at the present time is the most critical in the history of the mint, and the demand is increasing at a rate that has outstripped the capacity of both existing mints."[15]

Within two weeks the whole coinage problem was up for public discussion, and a new villain had been invented. "There is now," wrote Edward Cowan in the *New York Times,* April 5, "a serious shortage in the country of silver dollars and other coins. From the public's viewpoint, this is not yet acute. Apart from rare coin collectors, who have become more numerous in recent years, and piggy-bank savers, most people are not hoarding coins to protect themselves against scarcity. . . . Officials say that all coins are in short supply. The consensus is that the rapid expansion in coin-operated vending machines, laundries and parking meters is the cause." Arlen J. Large, writing in the *Wall Street Journal* early in April, drew the line from silver dollars to the coinage problem: "The Treasury's leisurely consideration of future coinage has become somewhat more urgent, however, because of last month's highly publicized raid by coin collectors on its supply of silver dollars."

But what of the new villain, the vending machine? It is hard to find a discussion of the coin shortage that does not point a finger of blame at the automatic coin-operated machines. They sell cigarettes, laundering, shoeshines, flowers, candy, hot soup. They gobble coin for telephone calls, turnpike passage, bridge tolls, tunnels, music, dry cleaning, parking. One authority estimates that they do an annual business of $4 billion in coin. But Mr. Thomas Hungerford, executive director of the National Automatic Merchandising Association, points out that the industry needs far less than that sum in circulating coinage. The industry thrives on high volume, fast turnover, and small profit margins. Coins left too long in the machines represent idle capital, and an all too easy target for vandalism. Every incentive drives the operator to empty his machines as often as possible. Hungerford estimates that the average machine is emptied 150 times a year. The industry as a whole, at any given moment, might not account for more than $22 million in coin outstanding.[16] And we have already noticed, above, that the automatic coin-operated machine has served as a *source* of coin during the shortage, and not as a sinkhole. The industry was an easily identified source of concentrated holdings of coin; because it would be affected deeply by any change in the coinage, the industry had every reason to cooperate with the authorities. In fact it did so, and there is good reason to suspect that the vending machines, when all is said and done, actually helped to alleviate the shortage. Miss Eva B. Adams, Director of the Mint, has disputed the idea that the coin-operated vendors are the villains. The fact is, says she, "that the vending machine people have been extremely cooperative in keeping coin in circulation."[17]

But the vending-machine theory will probably hang around to the bitter end. It is attractive, because it speaks in terms of machinery and technology, which is always fun, and which is especially convenient when a technical maladjustment in an unthinking mechanical complex is much more thinkable than, say, a broadly-based mass protest against debauching the currency.

To return to the question of "the cause" of the great coin shortage: another very popular "explanation" had to do with the rising population. Robinson and Young, authors of a book on the subject, put it this way: "The growth of the economy and population means more coins are needed by more people to carry out a greater number of retail sales. During the last decade the population of the United States has increased by about 30 million...."[18] Yes. But during the last decade the amount of subsidiary silver coinage outstanding has increased *even faster*—from $1.304 billion to $2.166 billion. A decade ago there was less coinage per capita. And no shortage. The population argument appears to be without force.

The most romantic explanation of the coin shortage appeared in a letter to the editor of *Barron's* from a certain Mr. Ralph Martin Shaw, who stoutly announced his thesis that "we are not short of coins due to hoarders or vending machines." Shaw continued: "The real reason for our shortage is the fact that U.S. coins are presently legal tender in all parts of the world. There are as many silver quarters in circulation in Italy as there are lira. The same is true of France and Spain. In some countries, there is no local currency. . . . In Egypt, our room boy asked me to convert some coins for him instead of a tip and I agreed. He produced $25 worth of quarters and dimes and I put them in circulation in the U.S. as a patriotic gesture. U.S. coins are acceptable in Australia, New Zealand, Thailand, Cambodia, Malaysia, India, Iran, the Near East, Europe, Africa, and South America."[19] How Mr. Shaw can count the silver quarters circulating in Italy, and also France, and also Spain, is beyond my ken; no doubt there are passages in his letter which he would soften on second thought. But there's every reason to believe in that Egyptian room boy with $25 worth of quarters and dimes.

There remain two possible sources of the difficulty: businessmen and speculators. It seems likely that businessmen in the retail field have been saving their coins rather than turning them in at the bank. This would be the prudent thing to do, in the absence of a general agreement among all the local retailers to turn their coin in. If the coinage has merely seeped out of the banks to be dammed up in the cash tills of retail businesses, then there is no public "shortage" actually, but only an abnormal distribution of the coinage. The banks will be short, but retailers will feel little pinch, and business will be very much as usual: so one might expect, on the assumption that the coinage will work just as efficiently as it did before. But it won't. The very essence of a banking system is efficient use of monetary resources—more efficient use than can be had by informal cooperation among the factors of production. Abolish, or bypass, the coin-handling function of the banking system, and it takes more coin to do the same work. There is a shortage. How much of the present shortage can be traced to prudential saving by retail businesses? No one knows. The Treasury did not direct its campaign at retail businessmen. It aimed at individual savers, and at children with piggy banks.

Could it be the speculators, then? Before taking a look at that question, it will be useful to "establish" one or two terms. People who hold an unusual quantity or value of coins may be divided into three groups. The hoarder is a Silas Marner, a Harpagon, the compulsive saver of coin; the miser; his type is definite but his numbers small; there could never be enough true hoarders to do damage to a major currency, unless some strange carrier should make this kind of derangement epidemic. For practical purposes the hoarder may be ignored. Next there is the genuine collector, the numismatist, who strives to build a collection of rare or beautiful or historic coins. The numismatist often exhibits an astounding erudition, perhaps because his success as a collector depends importantly upon his knowledge of a long and intricate historical development. Goethe is said to have recommended the perusal of beautiful medallions as a form of intellectual stimulation.[20] In 1850 there were only 300 coin collectors in the United States.[21] The present number of genuine collectors would probably not exceed the number of "mint sets" of coins sold each year by the Treasury. Each mint set contains specially polished coins, ten of them—one penny, one nickel, one dime, one quarter, one half from each mint (Denver and Philadelphia). Until recently, between 200,000 and 300,000 mint sets were sold each year. In 1963 the Treasury filled orders for 600,000 sets. By May of 1964 the Treasury had received orders for a million sets.[22] Even if we assume that there are as many as a million genuine numismatists, the arithmetic of the situation suggests that there would be little trouble to expect from their quarter. If each one of them had a collection of one thousand U.S. coins, the number of coins tied up in collections would amount to only 2 per cent of the outstanding U.S. coin circulation. That hardly seems to be a threat to the coinage.

Could it be the speculators, then? Not the hoarder, not the numismatist, but the speculator? I think so. I think it is highly likely that the strongest factor in the vanishing of the U.S. silver coinage is the factor of speculating against a rise in the price of silver. The price of silver is a result of the interplay of long-term trends in the supply of silver and the demand for it; I shall go into that question in some detail in a later chapter. It is enough, at this point, to suggest that the speculative element is the decisive one in the current coin shortage, because 1) all other possible "causes" of the shortage appear, on examination, to be insufficient explanations, and 2) the situation is the kind that seems classically irresistible to the speculator. The chance of profit is enormous if the price of silver goes up. The likelihood of a rise in the price of silver is something like 99.99 per cent. There is no risk if this forecast is wrong. A 50-cent piece can't be worth less than 50 cents.

And the explanation via speculation does satisfy the requirements of the situation. It would not require many speculators to offset the production of the U.S. mints. If there were a million speculators in 1964, and if each of them squirreled away one dollar's worth of silver coin per day, the entire output of the U.S. mints would not suffice to prevent a net shrinkage in the actually circulating coinage. The same would be true if each *household* in the country "saved" ten cents' worth of silver coin each *week*. The arithmetic is highly suggestive. The total circulation of subsidiary silver on September 30, 1965 came to $12.69 per person in the U.S., according to Treasury estimates.[23] That's only slightly more than one roll of quarters per person.

It could be argued that the present coin shortage is not serious, when compared with the historic shortages that have been experienced in these parts. As a matter of fact, the white man's civilization in North America has suffered from a shortage of coin for more than half of the time since the settlement of the Plymouth colony.[24] Adam Smith tells us that dried cod passed as money in Newfoundland, and sugar as money in several of the West Indian islands. Fish, "corn," and animal pelts were common coin among the early American colonists. "Corn" meant any sort of grain, including peas. The following sentences are from colonial decrees and court records of Massachusetts. "Sir Richard Saltonstall is fined four bushells of malte for his absence from Court" (September 28, 1630). "Chickataubott is fyned a skyn of beaver for shooteinge a swine of Sir Richard Saltonstall" (June 14, 1631). "It is ordered that corne shall passe for payment of all debts at the usuall rate it is solde for, except money or beaver be expressly named" (October 18, 1631). Hepburn points out that this last decree made "corne" full legal tender.

In and around Virginia, warehouse receipts for tobacco

stored in warehouses under the direction of the public authority circulated as money. No law made them legal tender. But they were backed by intrinsic value, and so possessed one of the characteristics of a good money. They circulated as money from almost the earliest times until just before the opening of the nineteenth century.

Black wampum (made from quohaug) and white wampum (made from periwinkle) circulated among the coastal Indians and eventually among the Dutch and English settlers. Several times the authorities had to "fix" the value of wampum by law. Massachusetts in 1643 made it legal tender for any sum not exceeding 40 shillings, counting 8 white beads to the penny and 4 black to the penny. In 1649 Rhode Island fixed the black wampum at the same level. But the art of making money by polishing beads appealed to the settlers, and by 1662 they had manufactured so much wampum that its usefulness was at an end. In 1662 Rhode Island refused to accept it in payment of taxes.

Although a mint was established in Boston in 1652 to coin silver (of sterling fineness) in 12d, 6d, and 3d pieces, and although laws were passed to prohibit the exportation of these coins, nothing remained of them by the middle of the eighteenth century. King Charles closed the mint in 1684 as an offense against his prerogative. The heaping issues of paper notes, repeatedly depreciating and being called in for redemption at sacrificial prices, drove out the sounder currency.

At the outbreak of the Revolutionary War, the amount of hard coin in the country was approximately $4 million. The population was 3,000,000. A sharp view of the coin shortage is presented in the journals of the charming Baroness von Riedesel, whose husband commanded the German troops who fought on the side of the British. The Baroness having been captured along with her husband and her children after the battle of Saratoga, she had an opportunity to observe the American officers, who, she noted, "set a great value upon our money coinage, which with them was scarce. One of our officers had worn his boots entirely into shreds. He saw that an American general had on a good pair, and said to him, jestingly, 'I will gladly give you a guinea for them.' Immediately the general alighted from his horse, took the guinea, gave up his boots, put on the badly-worn ones of the officer, and again mounted his horse."[25]

Between 1776 and 1780, large sums in good hard coin were spent by Britain and France on this side of the ocean, principally in prosecuting the war. By 1780 the supply of coin was abundant, France alone having spent $3 million here. Then the successive issues of "continentals," which rapidly became worthless, led to monetary chaos again. The Convention that eventually wrote the Constitution had been assembled originally for the restricted task of proposing solutions to a set of economic problems.

The new United States attempted to establish both gold and silver as full monetary metals. To do this required that the ratio of the weight of silver in a dollar to the weight of gold in a dollar should conform most exactly with the ratio of the respective prices per ounce in the open market. But the market ratio of course fluctuated. A gold coinage of $6 million had disappeared, almost all of it overseas, by 1821. The silver dollars minted before 1806 were of slightly lesser weight but remarkably finer appearance than the Spanish silver pesos circulating in the West Indies, although they traded without discount. So American dollars were converted to pesos, and the pesos were melted down and minted into a few more American dollars than one had started with. In 1806, to prevent further deterioration of the silver reserves, President Jefferson halted the minting of silver dollars. By 1853, according to Hepburn, "the country was denuded of silver, only the abraded foreign coins remaining in circulation. The inconvenience suffered by the public for want of small change became a crying evil, and Congress was impressed with the necessity for action." Thomas Corwin, Secretary of the Treasury, described the situation in January 1853: "This state of things has banished almost entirely from circulation all silver coins of full weight, and what little remains in the hands of the community consists principally of the worn pieces of Spanish coinage of the fractional parts of a dollar, all of which are of light weight, and many of them ten or twenty per cent below their nominal value."

Luckily, we struck gold. In 1824 a gold vein was opened in North Carolina. Not long afterwards gold was struck in Georgia. In 1835 mints were established at Dahlonega, Georgia, and Charlotte, North Carolina, and six states in the area were producing gold. The product came to $5,000 in 1824, $868,000 coined in 1832 and as much more uncoined, and $2 million in 1834. But it was impractical to coin gold in small denominations, and so the shortage of small coin persisted. The U.S. had to make do with that peculiar article, the fractional banknote. In the first decades of the nineteenth century the fractional banknotes were issued in denominations as small as three cents. Finally, in 1857, the Congress took a step towards providing a domestic currency: it deprived foreign coins of the legal tender status they had enjoyed since the founding of the Republic, allowing only Spanish-American fractional pieces to circulate, and that only for a limited purpose and during a limited period.

Another coin shortage developed during the Civil War,

following the passage of the Legal Tender Act, February 25, 1862. This act brought about an inflationary issue of "greenbacks," and the subsidiary silver coinage dropped out of circulation. Once more the peculiar makeshift was invoked; Congress authorized the issue of fractional paper banknotes ("shinplasters"). A more recent coin shortage in the U.S. was part of the worldwide reaction to the terrific rise in the price of silver during the First World War. Silver coins disappeared completely from circulation in many countries after the Armistice. For two months in 1919 the price of silver in New York was above the point at which it would start to be profitable to melt down silver dollars; for a brief period in November 1919 the price of silver threatened the subsidiary coinage. But no melting is known to have taken place. Perhaps it was widely suspected (and correctly) that the price of silver would be at that level only temporarily—not long enough, presumably, to allow even a fleet-footed speculator to arrange the massive transactions that would be necessary if anything but the most demure profits were to be realized.[26]

But the argument that we have had shortages in the past, and survived them, and therefore this present shortage can be shrugged off, ignores the great problems that can pop up in a highly mechanized society when the currency system gets out of whack. It is true that coin shortages are nothing new in American history. We have had shortages for more than half of the time we've been settling this country. In the midst of our desperate struggle for independence we had to get along with an indescribable chaos of currencies—the Spanish dollar and its "bits," the British coins, the French guinea and pistole, the Portuguese moidore and joe (Johannes), the Spanish doubloon and pistole, the French crowns and livres, and various understandings of the term "shilling," a Spanish dollar being valued at 6 shillings in New England and Virginia, 8 shillings in New York and North Carolina, 32½ in South Carolina, and 7½ in the remaining four colonies.

In the midst of that confusion there were calm hearts and clear heads at work fashioning a Constitution and establishing the beginnings of a national banking system. In the mid-1960's can we count on hearts as calm and heads as clear?

2. Silver: Supply and Demand

IT IS IN THE NATURE of silver to be the whitest of metals. There is no metal that has a higher or more lustrous reflectivity than silver. Paul Horgan captures the personality of silver when he speaks of the vessels used by the Spanish settlers of the upper Rio Grande four centuries ago: "Some of it was made in Spain, and bore Spanish hallmarks; much of it in Mexico. All of it was heavy, almost pure in its silver content and, except for any blazons of arms belonging to the family, plain. Light struck from its surface as from water, with a faint suggestion of ripple that added richness of texture to weight of substance."[1] The metal is not only beautiful, but it is also easily worked: only gold is more easily hammered into leaf or drawn filament.[2] It has been mined around the world, commonly enough to be useful and rarely enough to be seductive: necessary attributes of a monetary metal. Since the earliest times its qualities, like those of gold, have set it apart for purposes of coinage and art.

But the technological revolution has swept silver away from such tame domains, leaving gold in solitary authority in matters of coinage and adornment. Silver has new work to do, the kind of work that could have been invented only after a technological revolution had gone through its paces for a century or so. Silver, we learned finally, has the highest electrical conductivity of any metal. Silver has the highest thermal conductivity of any metal. It is next to gold in its resistance to corrosion. In combination with other elements, silver forms salts and compounds that have enormous importance in photography, medicine, and chemistry. The metal of coins and wedding plate has become the metal of photography and rockets. In 1928 the industrial (i.e., excluding art and jewelry) use of silver in the U.S. amounted to 14.7 million ounces. In 1964 it was 95.8 million ounces. The U.S. demand for silver in arts and industry averaged about 24 million ounces a year from the start of this century until 1941. Since 1941 there have been only seven years in which the U.S. demand for silver in arts and industry has been less than 100 million ounces.[3] It has exceeded 100 million ounces in every year since 1958.

The photographic industry is the most important industrial user of silver in the U.S. About 55 million ounces of silver are used each year in the silver nitrate compound (63.5 per cent silver) that provides the light-sensitivity that is essential to the photographic process. However, the concept of "use" requires careful defining when one is dealing with precious metals. It should be contrasted with "consumption." A precious metal may be said to have been consumed when it has been placed beyond any possibility of being used again as metal for any purpose. In this sense, the photographic industry consumes much less than the 55 million ounces of silver it uses each year. About 50 per cent of the silver on the negative of a black-and-white film is recovered in the developing of it. All of the silver on a color negative is replaced by dyes, and about 90 per cent of the silver is recoverable. The photographic industry actually consumes about 37 million ounces of silver a year.

Robinson and Young give a picture of very rapid growth in the use of silver for photographic purposes throughout the industrialized world. They note that in Canada photography pulled ahead of silverware in 1961 as a user of silver. Canadian demand for silver nitrate in 1961 was up 60 per cent from 1949. The industry grew 125 per cent in Great Britain from 1949 to 1958. From 1953 to 1959 the production of photosensitive goods expanded 130 per cent in West Germany, 57 per cent in France, 87 per cent in Italy, and at a comparable rate in Belgium and Japan.

The use of silver in electrical contacts is growing steadily. Silver is replacing copper not only because it is a better electrical conductor than copper, but because it is more reliable (and reliability is necessary in these days when machines are supposed to function millions of miles out in space). When copper contacts corrode, copper oxide is formed—an insulating material which cripples the contact. When silver contacts corrode, silver sulphide is formed—an electrical conductor that is not a bad substitute for silver itself. Silver is used in almost every on-off switch and can be found in almost every common electrical appliance, from mixmasters to electric blankets to electric toothbrushes. The highly educated gadgets used in aircraft and in the new telephone equipment are great users of silver contacts. Silver wire contact relays are at the heart of many a computer. About 28 million ounces of silver are currently being consumed in silver contacts each year in the U.S. Yes, consumed. There is little chance of recovery. The amount of silver in each contact is too small for economical recapture.

Another relatively new use of silver is in solders for brazing and bonding other metals. Robinson and Young quote "an authority" whom they leave unfortunately nameless: "Practically every end-product that has a joining or bonding problem is a potential user of silver solders. Where strong, ductile, corrosion-resistant joints are necessary and copper-alloy welding rods cause damage to the metal to be joined, process engineers specify and insist upon the use of silver solders." In such solders, alloyed with zinc, cadmium, lead, or copper, silver may range from 2.5 per cent to 98.5 per cent of the alloy. About 15 million ounces of silver are used yearly in solders in the U.S. It should be considered almost wholly consumed.

Silver-infiltrated tungsten has been used in rocket nozzles to handle the thermal shock of blast-off. Experts in rocketry are of opinion that once the rocket is in outer space the silver should be considered unrecoverable. Large amounts of silver are used, presumably in the bonding process, for the honeycomb structures in wing and empennage of jet aircraft. Detailed consumption figures are not available. However, Mr. John B. Stevens has mentioned that "missiles" accounted for the consumption of 200,000 ounces of silver in 1964.[4] And it is reported that in 1964 the Treasury sold 10 million ounces of silver to other government agencies "for defense purposes."[5] But there is no reason to assume that those 10 million ounces were used entirely in rocketry, or even in manufacturing.

One of the most rapidly growing new uses of silver is in batteries, a market that was opened up as late as 1957. Silver-zinc batteries can be recharged, they put out more juice than any other battery of similar weight and size, and they discharge at a constant voltage level. Silver-cadmium batteries are slightly heavier and more rugged; they are being used in portable television sets and in general wherever light weight is not the prime consideration. Once again the space and defense industries appear to be major users. The 1963 Explorer XVII satellite was reported to carry 150 pounds of silver-zinc batteries. The use of silver in batteries requires about 6 million ounces a year in the U.S.

Silver is also consumed in dentistry, medicine, the making of mirrors, the lining of corrosion-resistant vessels, and a multitude of minor objects and occasions. An approximate tabulation of the consumption of silver in industry in calendar 1964 in the U.S. is presented below:

U.S. Consumption
of Silver, 1964
(millions of ounces)

photographic	36.9
electrical	27.7
brazing, soldering	15.4
batteries	6.2
dental, medical	5.2
mirrors, vessels	3.2
miscellaneous	1.0
missiles	0.2
	95.8

A moment's reflection will persuade one that this represents a very special kind of demand in the market place. It is what the economists call "inelastic": the amount of silver bought and consumed for these purposes would be just about what it is now even if the price were twice the amount of the present price—or half of it. There are three occasions when "cost is no consideration," as the phrase goes. Cost is no consideration when the matter has to do with a strategic necessity in the national defense. Cost is no consideration when there is no known alternative. Cost is no consideration when the cost applies to an item that accounts for only a very small fraction of the final product. Most of the industries mentioned above exhibit these features. In the photographic industry, for example, the cost of silver amounts to approximately 3 per cent of total sales price to the public. If the price of silver were quadrupled, Eastman Kodak could pass the entire extra cost on to the final consumer by raising its prices merely 12 per cent. The photographic industry would just as soon pass on to its shareholders the profits that might arise if a cheap substitute for silver were available, however; and so there is a constantly building pressure to find just that. But it is easy to see that the photographic industry will continue to buy silver for almost any price during the next few years.* Its demand is almost as inelastic as the demand from strategic defense industries. Of all the uses mentioned above, only silver solders have exhibited a tendency to fall out of fashion when the price of silver rises (silver is a big part of the cost of the solder; and there are acceptable alternatives). Thus: *Perhaps 90 million ounces of silver would be consumed yearly in the U.S. no matter what the market price.*

One cannot understand what is happening in the silver market (or in the U.S. coinage) if one does not understand that sentence, and everything it implies. For this inelastic de-

---

*Joseph T. Morris, managing director of the National Association of Photographic Manufacturers, testified before the Senate Banking and Currency Committee on June 9, 1965, as follows: "There has been extensive research aimed at the development of substitutes for silver-based salts. This research has been accelerated within the past few years in part as a direct result of the substantial increase in the cost of silver which has occurred since 1961. Silver represents a considerable portion of the cost of sensitized photographic products. Yet, despite an increase in silver prices of over 40 per cent in the past four years, no acceptable substitute system has been devised and none is foreseeable."

mand for silver is a drastic departure from the historic pattern of the market. Silver appears to be one of the elements that are bearing the brunt of the technological revolution—along with the human personality. Each new development seems to open the door to a new use for silver, a new *consumption* of silver. That is why the irreducible minimum of silver consumption keeps rising. That is what lies behind those figures cited earlier, and repeated here: the U.S. consumption of silver in arts and industry averaged 24 million ounces a year from the start of this century until 1941. Since 1941 there have been only seven years in which the U.S. consumption of silver in arts and industry has been less than 100 million ounces. It has exceeded 100 million ounces in every year since 1958.

The reader may wonder why the table shown above comes to a total of 95.8 million ounces of silver consumed in the U.S. in 1964, although we have been talking upwards of 100 million ounces at the same time. The difference is in the use of silver for personal adornment and enjoyment: jewelry, flatware, and the arts. In 1964 approximately 27.2 million ounces were used in these pursuits in the U.S., bringing the total for "arts *and* industry" to 123.0 million ounces. But the silver that is demanded for silverware and jewelry is *not* consumed. It may form part of total demand one year but it does not form part of total consumption, because it could very well become part of total supply the next year. Silver plate can be melted. In foreign countries, in India *par excellence,* the silversmith and the melting pot are the principal conduits of private financial resources.

Up to this point I have been concerned to build a clear picture of the single most outstanding feature of the present silver situation: the great rise in the inelastic demand for silver that is destined to be consumed, to be used up beyond recovery. This is the central fact of the silver situation today. In order to get at it as directly as possible, I have delayed mentioning some further, and complicating, elements in the demand for silver.

There is, as we have just noted, a certain demand for silver to be used in jewelry and the arts. This demand is fundamentally different from the inelastic demand of modern industry. The demand coming from jewelry and the arts responds mercurially to changes in the price of silver; it responds indirectly to the ups and downs of the general economy; it represents silver that will not be consumed but will merely be "worked up" and then either displayed or stored; it tends to fluctuate with the marriage rate, in countries where it is customary to make wedding gifts of silver. In recent decades the amount of silver going into jewelry and the arts in the U.S. appears to have varied from a low of about 5 million ounces to a high of more than 60 million ounces. A "normal" year might see about 20 million ounces of silver going into jewelry and the arts. Perhaps the custom of giving silver to the bride is more restricted than I have supposed. Non-industrial demand for silver in the U.S. amounts to about 13 ounces per wedding.

Another element in the demand for silver is the coinage function of governments. The U.S. Government has coined silver almost continuously since 1789, and its coinage needs have been a major factor in the present re-ordering of the silver markets. With coinage demand, as with the demand from jewelers, it is important to remember that the silver that passes into these hands is not lost forever. Whenever the price is right, whole coinages are melted down for their bullion content. The mints can form part of the demand for silver, but they are not part of the consumption of silver. Coinage is a way-station between the silver mine and the ultimate consumer. A few private collectors and a few great museums may preserve samples of coinages into the indefinite future; but it is axiomatic that they preserve only those samples that have become rare because that coinage disappeared. No collector or group of collectors, official or unofficial, can preserve a whole coinage when the market says it would be profitable to melt it down.

In recent years the U.S. has converted a good deal of silver into coin:

U.S. Silver Coinage[5]
(millions of ounces)

1960	46.0
1961	55.9
1962	77.4
1963	111.5
1964	203.0

Finally, there is the overseas market. We have seen, above, that the consumption of silver in the photographic industry has grown rapidly in most of the industrialized countries of the Free World. Demand has grown just as rapidly in the electrical industries overseas. Many foreign countries mint a silver coinage; and every fourth year one country or another will burn up about 20 million ounces putting out a memorial medallion after the Olympics. Foreign countries are apparently much more interested in recoverable forms of silver: in 1964 they used almost 45 per cent of their silver acquisitions for jewelry and the arts, while the U.S. was using about 24 per cent.

It is possible, then, to build up an overall picture of the

current demand for silver in the Free World. Remember, in looking at these figures, that they represent many different kinds of demand, and that they can be added up together only because they pertain to the same metal; the economic meaning of an ounce of silver divagating through Cassiopeia is quite different from the meaning of an ounce of silver at work in a new computer.

The Use of Silver in the Free World
(millions of ounces)

	1964	1963	1962	1961	1960
Industry and Arts					
United States	123.0	110.0	110.0	105.0	100.0
Other Countries	162.9	142.2	137.8	134.5	124.6
	285.9	252.2	247.8	239.5	224.6
Coinage					
United States	203.0	111.5	77.4	55.9	46.0
Other Countries	61.5	55.5	50.2	81.2	57.9
	264.5	167.0	127.6	137.1	103.9
Grand Total	550.4	419.2	375.4	376.6	328.5

In 1964 approximately 100 million ounces of silver were used in the Free World for jewelry and the arts. Taking that sum away from the total amount used in the Free World, we can arrive at an estimate of the total inelastic industrial demand for silver in the Free World: about 185 million ounces. That figure is important as it stands; for we shall soon be comparing it with the total Free World production of silver. And the figure is disturbing, because it represents merely the 1964 level of a steadily growing consumption. The annual growth rate is probably in the neighborhood of 7 per cent.

Before leaving the matter of the demand for silver in the

U.S., it may be well to discuss a possible objection. It is commonly said (and I agree) that the U.S. demand for silver for industrial purposes is growing rapidly. If so, why has U.S. consumption in arts and industry been stagnant for twenty years? And then the figures are given:

U.S. Silver Consumption
in Arts and Industry
(millions of ounces)

1945	126.3
1950	110.0
1955	101.4
1960	102.0
1964	123.0

Certainly a superficial reading of those figures would satisfy anyone that there is little growth in the silver business. In this case the superficial reading is dangerously wrong. The 1945 figure represents the peak military consumption (in 1942, for example, the production of military insignia alone required 7 million ounces of silver). Through 1950 the pent-up demand for luxury goods was being satisfied in many ways —in a burst of buying silverware, among other things. Between 1937 and 1947 the dollar volume of silverware sales almost quadrupled, whereas the quantity of silver consumed in arts and industry grew not quite so fast. Since 1950 the price of silver and therefore the price of silverware have edged upwards; and since the demand for silverware is notably elastic, there has been a continuous pressure on sales. Alternatives, such as stainless steel, have steadily taken territory from the silversmiths. Meanwhile the use of silver in industry kept climbing, until in recent years the technological revolution took hold in a big way. A breakdown of the figures just cited will show the trend most clearly:

U.S. Silver Consumption	Arts	Industry
	(millions of ounces)	
1946	52	35
1950	63	47
1955	43	58
1960	28	74
1964	27	96

In the four years 1960-1964 the industrial use of silver grew by 30 per cent! That is an annual growth rate of about 7 per cent. It is applicable to the industrial portion of U.S. silver use, applicable therefore to 80 per cent of U.S. demand. And it is inelastic: insensitive to price. There is an imperiousness and power in this kind of demand, which will soon be felt perhaps throughout the world.

And what is there to meet this demand for silver? Two forms of the metal: 1) silver fresh from the mines—what is called "new production"; and 2) silver not freshly mined but available to the market anyway, as bullion or plate or coin.

New production of silver appears to have settled down on a plateau reached a generation ago:

	World Production of Silver[6] (millions of ounces)	New York Price Per Ounce
1900	180.9	$ .621
1910	234.5	.542
1920	173.2	1.019
1930	252.5	.385
1940	273.4	.348
1950	203.3	.742
1960	207.8	.914
1961	203.2	.924
1962	205.7	1.085
1963	213.1	1.279
1964	215.0	1.29+

I have added the average New York price of silver so that the remarkable lack of coordination between price and production can be seen. The silver market is indeed a special case: not only is *demand* inelastic, as we have already seen, but so is production. Since 1961 the market price of silver has risen 42 per cent, production 5 per cent, industrial demand 30 per cent! What goes on here?

The answer lies in the fact that very few mines are in business primarily to produce silver. Most of the silver comes from mines that are in the business of producing lead or zinc, copper or nickel—mines that consider silver a mere by-product. Only 3 per cent of all silver production comes from mines that are straight silver mines. Sixty per cent of the silver production comes from mines that get less than 40 per cent of their revenue from silver.[7] Clearly a rise in the market price of silver will not induce most mines to increase their tonnage of ore processing.

But when the price of silver goes up, isn't it true that a number of marginal mines that have been shut down will be opened up again and placed on stream? Robinson and Young show the calculations that go into a mining decision of this type. Since 1939 the price of silver has gone up, and labor costs have trebled. A mine that showed 5.34 ounces of silver per ton of ore earned enough revenue in 1939 to pay direct labor costs. In 1964 the ore would have to have 11 ounces of silver per ton, an extremely rich lode, to pay merely the labor costs. Such theoretical considerations are interesting, and in this case they are backed up by the drastic experience of recent years. There is no getting around the fact that the market price of silver rose 42 per cent, and silver production hiccoughed, yawned, and went back to sleep.

Other escape routes have been considered. There are some who have faith in Lady Luck. We will find a new

Potosí, they say. Others placidly await the announcement that some solitary inventor has discovered a way to mine ores so thin that they were never worked before. A few centuries ago such people would have subsidized the alchemists.

Actually no great new silver strikes should be expected. Back in December 1964 Mr. Robert Hardy Jr., Chairman of the Silver Committee of the American Mining Congress, announced that the outlook for silver production was upwards—modestly. Including the new mines in Ontario, Mr. Hardy looked forward to 38 million ounces of additional annual production by 1968. At the same time he admitted that some of the increased production of silver should be attributed to the rise in the market prices of—lead and zinc.

Those who hope to stumble on a vast new deposit of silver must reckon with a troublesome thing called the Epithermal Theory of Deposition. The long and the short of this theory (as it affects silver) is that the major silver deposits are to be found, by and large, at no great depth under the surface of the earth. The deeper you dig, the less you find. The ore gets thinner with depth. The mine "bottoms out." Silver is the opposite of gold in this respect. The great new gold strikes in South Africa were beyond the reach of the miners of yesterday who could not sink a mine shaft two miles into the earth. It is not impossible that the first mine to hit a depth of five miles will strike even more gold. It is not foolish to think that a great deal of gold remains to be discovered and brought to market. As to silver, it does not seem foolish to assert that the great strikes were made years ago. Although there is always Antarctica...and the silver in the water of the oceans....

As to the production of silver in the U.S., already included in the world figures given above, here is a summary for recent decades:

U.S. *Silver Production*
(millions of ounces)

1900	57.6
1910	57.1
1920	55.4
1930	50.6
1940	68.3
1950	42.3
1960	36.8
1961	34.9
1962	36.3
1963	35.0
1964	36.0

Here the situation is more grotesque than in world production. In the recent period when the price of silver was rising 42 per cent, American silver production actually dropped a bit. Almost 70 per cent of U.S. silver is brought to the surface as a by-product of other mining operations. Only four of the top 25 U.S. silver mines derive their principal revenue from silver. In 1963 some 30 per cent of U.S. silver production was a by-product of copper mining, 12 per cent a by-product of lead mining, 5 per cent a by-product of zinc, and 20 per cent a by-product of complex ores (combinations of copper, lead, zinc). Silver is mined in Alaska, Arizona, California, Colorado, Idaho, Michigan, Missouri, Montana, Nevada, New Mexico, South Dakota, Tennessee, Utah, and Washington—fourteen states. That means 28 United States Senators. Silver, which accounts for the merest fraction of total United States mining business, has a sentimental or political influence upon 28 per cent of the United States Senate.

Just as it was necessary to distinguish between use and consumption, so on the production side of the business it is necessary to distinguish between "production" and "supplies."

Obviously something more than new production is coming to market to satisfy demand if, in 1964, the Free World used 550.4 million ounces of silver while producing only 215.0 million ounces. What makes up the difference is previously mined silver that has been used but not consumed: silverware, bullion hoards, coinage. The entire economic life of silver can be schematized as follows:

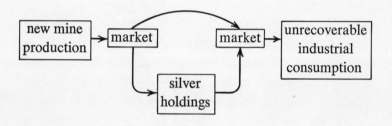

Observe that there are two points of competition. At the mine head there are two takers for the new production. At the edge of the abyss, where silver is swallowed up beyond recovery, there are two sources ready to offer silver. Of course there are subsidiary competitive markets within each major factor in the system. Mines compete with each other. Hoarders of coin compete with the government. The silverware manufacturers compete with the photographic industry. But these internal competitions are tautological, from the longer-range point of view.

This sketch of the economic life of silver doesn't differ from the sketch that might be made for almost any metal—with the single exception of gold, which can be "consumed" only by catapulting it into outer space. What makes the silver market extraordinarily different from other metal markets is, of course, the presence of government as a major element in the intermediary position. Government is powerful over a short span of time. For the short pull it is more powerful than any single factor in an economy. If the government wishes to be favorable to the silver miners, it can purchase silver at a price above the market price. For a short period the miners· prosper, and the silver piles up in government hoards. Ultimately the silver must be got rid of, and when the government offers it on the market the effect is to depress the market price. Then for a short time the users of silver are favored. The whole transaction, when viewed from a sufficient distance so that both sides of it come into perspective, appears to have accomplished nothing. And that is true, but it is not the whole story. The government has not mined any silver that wouldn't eventually have been mined. It hasn't sold any silver that wouldn't eventually have been sold. The favors it showed to the miners at the beginning are shown to the users at the end. Apparently everyone comes out even. But no. During the entire period of artificial pricing, a degree of inefficiency affects the market because the use of capital and the consumption of natural resources are not directed by economic forces. They are not directed by the forces of economizing. To some immeasurable extent there has been a waste of resources. In this case a very precious commodity, silver, is being wasted because the U.S. Government makes it available at a price that is far below the price it might command in a free market. The Treasury's reasons for doing this will be the subject of the next chapter. Here we are concerned with the Treasury's position in the supply side of the silver market, which is best shown in tabular form.

The Silver Market:
Supply and Demand in the Free World
(millions of ounces)

Demand	(est.) 1965	1964	1963	1962	1961	1960
Industry & Arts	305	285.9	252.2	247.8	239.5	224.6
Coinage	365	264.5	167.0	127.6	137.1	103.9
Hoarding	100	70.0	)		75.0	
Total	770	620.4	419.2	375.4	451.6	328.5

Supply						
New Production	225	215.0	213.1	205.7	203.2	207.8
Melted Coin	20	20.0	15.0	20.0	30.0	10.0
Salvage	15	11.4	4.4	6.9	29.0	21.5
Dishoarding	50	20.0	50.0	39.5	15.9	12.0
U.S. Treasury	460	354.0	136.7	78.3	118.5	67.5
Total	770	620.4	419.2	350.4	396.6	318.8

In 1960, 1961, and 1962, the difference between supply and demand was made up by sales of silver by Communist China. These sales were for the purpose of securing Western exchange with which to pay for the wheat that was shipped to Communist China following extremely poor harvests. The Communists explained that the weather was to blame. Actually the "Great Leap Forward" was a major factor in sapping the Chinese peasants of their customary zeal in farming. The results of the severe communalization of the farmers were not much different in Communist China from the results of communal farming in Governor Bradford's Plimoth Plantation. Weather, however, has been a major factor in setting world silver prices in the past. For many years the monsoons of India dictated the New York price of silver, and did so until at least 1914.[8]

Lest the tabulation of world supply and demand be misunderstood, I should explain that the term "hoarding" used there refers to speculative buildup of inventories and also to plain speculation in the silver market. Also it may be noticed by experts that the sums given as the yearly declines in U.S. Treasury stocks of silver are slightly different from the sums that can be derived by working with the year-end Treasury figures for bullion and free silver. These slight differences arise from the estimates that are used for coinage melting and dishoarding. The estimates are those of Handy & Harman (except 1965, which I have estimated). Indeed, the 1964 Annual Review of the silver market, published by Handy & Harman, exhibits the same statistical discrepancies. On pages 19 and 20 they publish figures that indicate the Treasury silver stock declined by 354.0 million ounces in 1964. On page 22 they publish a different set of figures that show the Treasury lost 349.5 million ounces in 1964. The statistics on silver have always been slippery.

In my estimates of 1965 supply and demand I have applied a 10 per cent growth rate to the industrial portion of "industry and arts" and have assumed that the "arts" portion will remain stable. The coinage estimate assumes stable coinage in foreign countries and U.S. silver coinage at levels predicted by the Treasury itself. I have assumed a slight increase in speculative hoarding as a result of the much greater publicity the silver problem has been receiving.

A perusal of the tabulation will show how important the U.S. Treasury has become in the silver market. It is supplying twice as much silver as is being mined in the whole Free World. In the first six years of the 1960s the Treasury will have supplied more than 1.2 billion ounces of silver to the world silver market—equivalent to the total world production of silver in the entire seventeenth century, the epoch of great production after the conquests of Mexico and Peru. The silver market as we know it today is an extension of the U.S. Treasury. The crucial fact is that the Treasury must very soon stop selling its silver at the current price. At the end of 1964 the Treasury stock of silver bullion was 1,208.2 million ounces. It had dropped by 23 per cent in 1964. In 1965 it continued to drop, but at a rate of 36 per cent yearly—another instance, perhaps, of acceleration towards the end of a monetary cycle.

If there is no further acceleration, the Treasury will have entirely exhausted its stock of silver by mid-1967. But we have seen that silver is rapidly becoming a metal of military significance. The U.S. consumed 500 million ounces of silver during the second World War and used more than 400 million ounces, in addition, as loans to our allies to aid them in their war production. A prudent government would want to have at least that much silver on hand in case another war requiring major military production should break out. Or calculate it from the production side. In a major war we should not count on receiving silver from mines outsides the Western Hemisphere. Luckily this hemisphere produces the bulk of the world's silver. In 1964 Canada produced 31 million ounces, Mexico 41 million, Peru 37 million, and the U.S. 36 million. Western Hemisphere production, total, was 159 million ounces. If in a future war we shall need 300 million ounces a year, then we should start the war with silver reserves equivalent to 150 million ounces for each year the war is expected to last. In that case the present silver stocks of the Treasury would last six years, assuming they were devoted entirely to war purposes. It is difficult to avoid the conclusion that we are dipping into strategic military reserves at this moment, and have been doing so since the beginning of 1965 —and all because the Treasury wants to keep the market price of silver below $1.29 per fine ounce.

3.   Silver and the U. S. Treasury

SILVER COIN HAS its beginning in Asia Minor, around 2,600 years ago.[1] There the Lydians stamped their lumps of precious metal to certify their weight and fineness. The lumps of metal came from the golden sands of the river Pactolus, which flowed through the capital city, Sardis. The metal was a natural alloy of silver and gold, later called *ēlektron* by the Greeks and *electrum* by the Romans. Thus at the very beginning of monetary history the two principal monetary metals, gold and silver, are found united in a bimetallic standard. For the next 2,600 years no effort has brought more grief to government and citizen than the hopeless effort to keep gold and silver circulating simultaneously as full legal tender.

The Greek and Latin word for this alloy was a metaphorical name. *Electrum* meant "amber." It was applied to the gold-silver alloy because that alloy had the color of amber. Amber had been known from immemorial antiquity. As early as 1,600 B.C. the trade routes from the Baltic Sea to the Adriatic and down the western coast of Greece were thick with the flow of amber to the Mediterranean. The trade continued for 2,000 years. Thus the silver drachma of the Greeks found its way to Northern Europe. Some 350 caches of Roman coins have been discovered in the coastal homeland of the ancient Balts. They treated coin as an ornament, perhaps as a lucky token, and buried it with its owner.[2]

The electrical property of *electrum* (amber) had been known from ancient times. Pliny the Elder describes this and the other notable qualities of amber, in his *Natural History,* with a tone of high satisfaction. Dr. Johnson rises almost to poetry in the article on amber in his *Dictionary*.

The Greeks caught up the idea of a circulating money and took it, as they took whatever they set their mind to, to a high degree of excellence. Groseclose points out that the Greeks made only one attempt throughout their history to "experiment" with inflated currency. Otherwise they voted overwhelmingly for sound money. There seems to be no doubt that the soundness of the Greek currency was an essential element in Greek commercial predominance. The conquests of Alexander introduced the silver drachma to the lands of Asia, and silver remains to this day the preferred monetary metal in most of Asia. By the first century A.D., Rome was importing silk, spice, jewels, and artifacts from the East at the rate of 100,000,000 sesterces a year—which Brooks Adams converted (in 1896) to $4 million dollars.[3] In terms of the debased dollar of 1965, the equivalent would be in the neighborhood of $40 million. And that was in silver paid to Arabia and India alone.

The precious metals flowed out of late Rome in payment of imports and in full flight from the growing economic chaos. Diocletian's famous attempt to decree the prices of some 900 items of goods and services failed. Groseclose tells the story of the next centuries succinctly:

The price fixing decree of Diocletian was a failure, and was abandoned within five years. It cast economy into too rigid a mold, and the result was, in the West, at least, only crystallization, disintegration. From the crisis of the third century, the Western Roman Empire never recovered. By the fourth century money had fallen to the degraded position of *ponderata,* when it was customary to assay and weigh each piece. And by the seventh century, the weights themselves had been so frequently degraded that it was no longer possible to make a specific bargain for money. There was no law to define the weight of a pound or an ounce, and no power to enforce the law if one existed. Under these circumstances money became extinct.[4]

In all of Europe, in the year 806 A.D., there was only £35 million worth of the precious metals.[5] There was probably not much change in this figure until the discovery of America. What the mines of the New World meant to Europe can be measured by comparing that £35 million with the world production of precious metals in the ensuing centuries. From 1493 to 1600, world production of gold and silver amounted to £290 million. Gold and silver worth £460 million were produced in the seventeenth century, gold and silver worth £730 million in the eighteenth century.

Three centuries before the discovery of America, the sack of Constantinople led to the decline of the Eastern Empire and the disappearance of its wonderful currency, the bezant, from widespread foreign circulation. The bezant had kept its metallic weight and fineness for 800 years, contributing mightily to the commercial preeminence of the Eastern Empire. After 1204 A.D. the center of finance moved west, spreading from Venice across Europe. In the opening years of the thirteenth century one of the new silver mines being worked in Europe was in Joachimsthal, Bohemia. In 1517 the mine at Joachimsthal began to coin its silver into a piece weighing well over 400 grains. Although this was not the first silver coin of this size struck in quantity (the first was the Saxony flap-hat of about 1500), it appears to have been the first of its type to achieve a great circulation. The coin became known as the Joachimsthaler, and eventually as the thaler or taler, daler, and of course dollar. After the discovery of the rich silver mines in Mexico and Peru, the Spanish authorities minted silver in the New World in a coin weighing 423.7 grains. This peso, being similar in size and weight to the Joachimsthal dollar, became known as the "Spanish dollar." It was struck in immense quantity, and huge sums of Spanish dollars came to circulate in the American colonies. They came in through American colonial trade with the Spanish West Indies and also through the free-spending hands of the freebooters who preyed on the treasure ships bound for the Spanish homeland. At the time of American independence, the Spanish dollar was the most common coin in circulation in the colonies. The paper money "continentals" issued by the Continental Congress during the Revolutionary War were denominated in dollars. Thomas Jefferson recommended that the unit of currency in the new United States be named the dollar. In 1792 Alexander Hamilton recommended that the dollar be coined at 416 grains, in accord with the weight of the average Spanish dollar then circulating. The Spanish dollar was full legal tender in the U.S. until 1857. The U.S. silver dollar, with only minor alterations, remained in circulation until 1964. That, in very rough outline, is the story of silver coin up to the administration of President Washington. The new government of the United States merely adopted the existing coin without repudiating gold, and so it came about that we were on a bimetallic standard. Silver and the U.S. Treasury have a long (and not always lustrous) historical connection.

Initially there was the problem of the coinage ratio. This is also known as the mint ratio, the legal ratio, mint rate, or coinage rate. It is the ratio of the weight of silver per monetary unit to the weight of gold per monetary unit. Obviously if both metals existed in the same quantity and were mined in the same quantities and were regarded as interchangeable by the general public, then the monetary unit could be defined legally as a certain ounceage of one or the other metal. But if the metals exist in different quantities (they do) and are mined at different rates (they are) and are regarded by the general public in different terms (they are), then an ounce of one is worth more or less than an ounce of the other. Here is the problem the government cannot solve. On the one hand it has to define the currency by law as such-and-such weight of gold or silver (we are describing the bimetallic standard). On the other hand it has to amend that definition almost daily as the market valuations of the two metals fluctuate. If the law is amended too frequently, then the law has no permanence and serves as only a shaky basis for private contracts. But if the law is held rigid in the face of fluctuating market ratios, then one or the other coin will disappear. Such has been the experience ("Gresham's Law") of every nation that has tried to maintain the bimetallic standard.

Brooks Adams tells us, for example, that the market ratio of silver to gold was 8.9 in 47 B.C. (Caesar had introduced gold coinage in Rome), 9.3 in 1 A.D. under Augustus, 9 to 10 from 100 to 200 A.D., Trajan to Severus; 12.5 in 310 under Constantine, and 18 in 450 under Theodosius.[6] Europe moved from a barter economy to a money economy after the great mines of the New World were opened, but the mint ratio remained to harass the governors. The production ratio was changing:

World Production of Precious Metals
(millions of ounces)

	Gold	Silver
1493–1600	23	747
1601–1700	29	1,272
1701–1800	61	1,833

In 1663 the English guinea (made from gold mined in Guinea, West Africa) was fixed at 20 shillings silver. Later it passed for 30 (debased) shillings. Towards the end of the century the rate was set at 22 shillings, then at 21½; and in 1717 at 21 shillings. That ratio reflected the report prepared by Sir Isaac Newton for the Royal Mint in 1717, wherein the great scientist asserted a historical production ratio of 15:1 and recommended a mint ratio of 15:1. It was this ratio that Alexander Hamilton recommended at the founding of the U.S. monetary system.

Unfortunately, silver production immediately started rising and gold production fell. The market ratio, which had been close to 15 in 1792 when Hamilton made his recommendations, reached 15.74 in 1799 in Europe, and varied between 15.5 and 16 for the next fifty years. By 1810 our currency was almost entirely silver; gold was being exported. Congress had to start amending the monetary law: it changed the mint ratio to 16.002 in 1834 and to 15.988 in 1837. Then between 1840 and 1860 the great gold strikes were made in California, Australia, and Russia. The market ratio dropped from 15.7 in the 1840s to 15.3 in the 1850s. By 1853 the U.S. (which was still insisting on a mint ratio of 15.988) was suffering from a severe shortage of subsidiary silver coin. In effect the U.S. had been on a single gold standard for many years. In 1853 the Congress stopped the free minting of subsidiary silver and reduced slightly the silver content of the subsidiary coins, limiting them at the same time to legal tender for debts not exceeding $5. The free minting of silver dollars was maintained, but none was minted, because the market value of the bullion content of the silver dollar remained above $1.00. In the 1850s certain influential economists in France and England were thinking of going onto a full silver standard, demonetizing gold entirely. In 1859 the Holyoke Water Power Company negotiated a contract payable in "ounces troy weight of silver." Such was the prestige of the metal at that time.

But the vicissitudes of bimetallism are endless. In the 1860s and 1870s gold production tapered off again; in 1858 the fabulous (silver) Comstock Lode had been turned up in Nevada. By 1873 the Congress had had enough of bimetallism, and the Coinage Act of February 12, 1873, placed the U.S. for all practical purposes on the gold standard; under this act only gold enjoyed free coinage.

Coinage of the United States

	Gold	Silver Dollars	Subsid. Silver
1793–1833	$ 11,825,890	$1,439,517	$34,835,561
1834–1848	64,512,740	954,873	36,257,043
1849–1873	775,775,807	5,636,848	67,141,057

The action of the U.S. Congress in 1873 was part of a worldwide turn towards gold. Portugal had adopted the gold standard in 1854. Germany went on gold in 1871, and her example was influential in the climate of awe that followed her brilliant conduct of the Franco-Prussian War. In 1878 the Latin Monetary Union (France, Belgium, Switzerland, Italy) stopped the free coinage of silver and went on the "limping" gold standard *(étalon boiteux)*: that is, there was free coinage of gold, but the government was not obliged to redeem in gold the outstanding silver currency. In 1873 Denmark and Sweden formed the Scandinavian Monetary Union (which Norway joined later) and went on the gold standard. By 1875 the Netherlands had completed the switch from silver to gold. Free coinage of silver stopped in Russia in 1876, in Spain in 1878, in Austria-Hungary in 1879. By 1880 no mint in Europe would accept silver for free coinage. But, because of the silver coins still in circulation, most of the European countries would still have to be described as being on the *étalon boiteux*. India and China remained on silver, continuing the preference they had shown for that metal since they first dealt in the drachmas of Alexander and the pesos of Mexico.

Thus there was a swiftly declining demand for silver as coinage metal. In the midst of this declining demand there was an enormous increase in silver production; and during the 1860s and 1870s gold production fell off. The average annual world production of silver was 25 million ounces in the 1840s, 40 million in the 1860s, 70 million in the 1870s, 100 million in the 1880s, and 160 million ounces in the 1890s. Before 1860 the U.S. had produced a small fraction of 1 per cent of the world's silver; in the 1860s it produced 20 per cent; in the 1870s and 1880s, 40 per cent. Between 1873 and 1876 the price of silver fell drastically. There were then, as always, two solutions to the economic problem: the genuine, free-market solution; and the pseudo-solution of governmental intervention. Had the free-market solution been chosen, production would eventually have declined to the low level of demand for silver in jewelry and the arts; and the vast stores of the Comstock Lode might have been saved for that day, not too distant, when silver would gain importance as an industrial and strategic metal. But the U.S. chose the route of governmental intervention, for which the price is now, after a long delay, being paid.

Back in the 1840s most of the silver produced in the U.S. was produced in territories, not states. But the political power of the silver areas gained rapidly as the silver areas became full-fledged members of the Union. California joined the Union in 1850. Nevada became a state in 1864. Colorado joined up in 1876. Montana, South Dakota, and Washington joined in 1889. Idaho joined in 1890, Utah in 1896. In the decades when silver was losing in the marketplace it was gaining 16 spokesmen in the U.S. Senate. And in the wave of Western resentment of Eastern "bloated bondholders" after the Civil War, the House of Representatives gained many Western members who reflected a popular prejudice for monetary inflationism.

The Coinage Act of 1873 now came to be called "the crime of '73" by those who favored silver (and who didn't stoop to explain where *they* were when the great crime was perpetrated). In the 44th Congress (1875-1877) a bill for the free coinage of silver was introduced by Rep. Richard P. ("Silver Dick") Bland of Missouri. President Hayes opposed the inflationists; Treasury Secretary John Sherman favored payment of all bonds in gold. Sen. William B. Allison of Iowa greatly altered the Bland scheme. The Bland-Allison Silver Purchase Act was vetoed by President Hayes and was passed over his veto on February 28, 1878. Thus the U.S. continued, after 1878, on the *étalon boiteux*. Under the Bland-Allison Act the Treasury purchased between $2 million and $4 million of silver per month at the going market price. But the market price was determined to drop. So in 1890 the Congress repealed the Bland-Allison Act and passed the Sherman Silver Purchase Act of 1890. This authorized the Treasury to purchase 4.5 million ounces of silver per month at the going market price. The Congress had overlooked the fact that the country was still on the gold standard; the Treasury notes backed by the new silver purchases kept being redeemed at the Treasury in gold; the heavy drain on gold threatened the solidity of the whole monetary structure. In 1893 the Sherman Act was repealed in turn. Approximately 387 million silver dollars (the "Morgans") were struck between 1878 and 1904. With the opening of South African mines in the latter half of the 1890s, gold production started rising (as had been correctly forecast during the early 1890s and ignored by the Silver Democrats, Bryan included, during the 1896 campaign). In 1900 silver was no longer an issue, and in 1904 the Democratic Presidential candidate was Alton B. Parker, a Gold Democrat. On March 14, 1900, the Congress passed the Gold Standard Act, fixing the dollar at 25.8 grains of gold %10 fine. By 1914 only China and a few minor countries remained on a silver standard.

In April 1918 Senator Key Pittman of Nevada introduced a bill to melt 350 million silver dollars and sell the silver to help India (where gold wouldn't circulate; the people clamored for silver rupees). Senator A. B. Fall of New Mexico tacked on an amendment that provided for the repurchase (at $1 the ounce) of an equivalent supply of silver from "domestic" mines and reducers. The Pittman Act became law on April 23, 1918. Under this demented legislation the Mint immediately began melting silver dollars. By May 1919 it had melted 259,121,554 "Morgan" dollars, and sold the metal to Britain for the Indian monetary system. Concurrently the Mint melted 11,111,168 more silver dollars for re-use as subsidiary silver. In 1919 the Treasury and Federal Reserve handed over to American bank branches in the Orient a batch of 29 million silver dollars to be sold in the Orient in an attempt to hold the market price of silver *down*. At the same time, under the Pittman Act, the Government was purchasing 200 million ounces of silver to keep the price *up*. Nevertheless the price fell. Governments neither create nor correct. They can disturb the effects of the free market; they can defer the effects of the free market; but in the long run the free market has its way. Its way is made smoothest if it is allowed to make its own delicate corrections day by day, hour by hour.

Almost simultaneously with the melting of silver dollars, the Government started minting them. These were the Peace dollars, celebrating the end of the first World War. Between 1921 and 1935 the Mint struck 191 million of these silver dollars. Silver hit its all-time low market price in 1932. It was 14 more years before silver production bottomed out.

Between 1919 and 1933, some 33 countries reduced the silver content of their coinage, and six countries abandoned silver entirely.

The example of free market adjustment in the lead trade after the first World War is a brilliant contrast. Benjamin Anderson tells the episode dramatically:

The Government controls promptly relaxed, but in a good many cases prices remained fixed by informal agreement among producers. In one such case the fixed price was held despite a drastic reduction in demand. One great smelting company had a contract to take and refine all the lead that a number of important mines could produce. It was being overwhelmed by the lead which they were producing and which it was unable to dispose of at a fixed price. The company thereupon notified the other interested firms that the next morning, beginning at nine o'clock, it was going to sell lead, and was going to make a price that would move the lead. What that price would be it did not know. The other companies felt that the great smelting company was very decent to give them advance notice and stood aside and watched the procedure. The next morning lead was down ¼ ¢, down another ¼ ¢, down another ¼ ¢, the reduction finally amounting to 4½ ¢ with no increase in buying. Another ¼ ¢ reduction met some speculative buying. The selling company promptly raised its price ¼ ¢ and then encountered trade buying. It raised its price another ¼ ¢ and the trade buying fell off. It dropped its price ¼ ¢ and the trade buying was resumed. Then the other companies got into the game and began to sell lead, and a free and open competitive market was established at which lead moved within a range of ½ ¢ at about 4½ ¢ below the previously prevailing price. The reduced price discouraged lead production. Supply and demand were equated. Right prices are prices that move goods. Right prices cannot be foreseen in advance. They must be found out experimentally in the open market.[7]

Fifteen years after the Pittman Act of 1918 became law, Senator Pittman was a member of the American delegation to the World Economic Conference in London. In 1918 Senator Pittman had successfully advocated the melting of 350 million U.S. dollars to be shipped to India. Now India was selling silver. At the London conference Senator Pittman helped the U.S. negotiate an agreement among the chief users and producers of silver, according to which India would limit her sales of silver to 35 million ounces a year, and the major producing countries would absorb the same amount of silver per year and keep it off the market for four years. The American share was 24,421,410 million ounces per year. The Pittman agreement under which India would dump slowly upon us the Pittman silver we had dumped rapidly upon her was considered a Pittman triumph.

But this was only the beginning of an amazing period for

silver and the Treasury. In December 1933, when the domestic market price of silver was 43¢ an ounce, President Roosevelt issued an executive order authorizing the Mint to pay, in effect, 64.64¢ an ounce to domestic producers of silver. This order was issued under the authority of the Thomas Amendment to the Agricultural Adjustment Act of May 1933, introduced by the great inflationist, Senator Elmer Thomas of Oklahoma. On June 19, 1934, the Congress passed the Silver Purchase Act, which gave the Secretary of the Treasury almost unlimited authority to buy and sell silver at home or abroad, the ostensible purpose being to increase the official holdings of silver until they should equal one-third the gold stock (valuing silver at $1.29 an ounce and gold at $35 an ounce). In August 1934 the President, acting under powers given him in the Silver Purchase Act, ordered all silver in the continental U.S. to be delivered to the Government within 90 days (except coins, silver held for industrial use, and various other major categories such as fabricated articles, silver owned by a foreign government or central bank, silver below .800 fine and not in use; silver held under license; silver mined after December 21, 1933); for this silver the Government would pay 50.01¢ an ounce. About 109 million ounces were received in the first 90 days and 4 million ounces more before the order was rescinded in 1938. Benjamin Anderson speaks darkly of some huge private gains made by insiders who knew the course of silver legislation. A special surtax of 50 per cent was slapped on all silver dealings. On August 9, 1934, the last silver contracts were liquidated on the New York Commodity Exchange—at 49.96¢, .999 fine. The private market for silver in the U.S. came to an end. A silver futures market opened in Montreal on October 22 and one in London opened on May 1, 1935.

After 1934 the Treasury was acquiring silver under five different programs and always at different prices for each program. It received war-debt silver in 1934 at 50¢ an ounce. It bought newly mined domestic silver under the Presidential order of December 21, 1933, at prices ranging from 64.64¢ to 74.72¢ from 1934 to 1938. It paid from 50.01¢ to 50.03¢ for nationalized silver. It paid from 44.80¢ to 63.82¢ for silver bought under the Silver Purchase Act of 1934. It paid between 43.80¢ and 53.94¢ for silver contained in gold bullion deposits and miscellaneous. The Treasury issued only the most sketchy and irregular reports on its silver purchases. It was not until July 1938 that the Treasury began to report regularly on the ounceage as well as the dollar value of each class of silver listed in the "Daily Statement."

If anyone has ever provided a full explanation of the objectives of the Roosevelt Administration's silver policy, it has been kept well hidden. The most coherent explanation is that the entire thing was a vast hoax: a method of inflating the currency while giving the impression that every new dollar was fully backed by good silver. Nevertheless, the Roosevelt Administration pursued its intricate and inexplicable silver policy over the objections of foreign diplomats and to the ruin of more than one foreign currency.

Foreign markets had begun to reflect the artificial pricing of the U.S. Treasury. By early 1935 the foreign market for silver hit 55¢ an ounce. In mid-February it rose again. On April 10, 1935, it reached 64.125¢. That day, at noon, Secretary of the Treasury Morgenthau told the press that the Government would meet the world price whatever it might be. That evening the President was forced to amend his proclamation, adjusting the price, in effect, to 71.11¢. In two days the world price hit 68.5¢. On April 24 it hit 71.625¢. Roosevelt and Morgenthau conferred, and President Roosevelt issued still another proclamation, April 24, raising the Treasury's buying price to 77.57¢. The world market banged through to 77¢ the next day and 81¢ the day after that. The Treasury at this point ceased its aggressive buying on the foreign market and refused to raise its price. The market held above 70¢ through June 1935 and fell to 67.75¢ by August 12. But on August 14 the Treasury, pegging the price at 65.375¢, was required to take 25 million ounces. The Treasury held this price until December 7, 1935. (That was a Saturday. Almost every major monetary decision is made on a weekend.) On Monday, December 9, it suddenly became clear, though no announcement was made, that the Treasury had abandoned its silver buying policy. No announcement ever was made. No explanation has ever been given. Within two weeks the price of silver fell to 49.75¢. On January 20, 1936, the price dropped to 44.75¢. It held at that price for the next ten years, with the exception of three years (1939 to 1942) when it traded between 35¢ and 40¢. In the 12 months *before* the Roosevelt Administration started intervening in the silver market, the New York price for silver had climbed from the depression low of 24¢ to 42¢ all by itself in the free market.

It has been said that one objective of the Roosevelt silver policy was to help China. The price of silver had been depressed. China possessed a huge stock of silver. China could buy more in world markets if her silver were valued higher. But this explanation is questionable, because China herself expressed concern over the possibility of U.S. intervention as early as 1933; towards the end of 1933 China let it be known she was opposed to any artificial rise in the price of silver. Early in 1934 she expressed serious concern over the prospects of U.S. silver legislation. The Silver Purchase Act of 1934 was passed on June 19. In June some 13 million Chinese Standard silver dollar were exported. In July, 24 million C.S. silver dollars were exported. In August, 79 million C.S. silver dollars were exported. The August 22 editorial in *Finance & Commerce,* a weekly published in Shanghai, cut to the bone of the matter: "...the existing position [of China] is one of extreme difficulty and danger. That it has been created entirely by the steps taken in another country to satisfy, from political motives, a craving for experiment, makes it no easier to bear." On August 19, 1934, the Chinese Minister of Finance, Dr. H. H. Kung, sent a message of alarm to President Roosevelt, asking the U.S. to explain its silver policy "in order that China may properly safeguard her currency." The U.S. greatly delayed its answer. Not until October 12 did it reply to China's emergency request. And then it was merely a laconic telegram from Secretary of State Cordell Hull, explaining that the President was carrying out the provisions of the Silver Purchase Act of 1934. On October 14, China took steps in tax and tariff policy to halt the silver outflow. The lack of free movement of silver between China and the world divorced the C.S. dollar from the world silver price; and so China in effect was off the silver standard.

The new Chinese taxes and tariffs put an end to official exports of silver. But China has a long coastline, and smuggled exports took over where the officials left off. In 1933 China exported 11 million ounces of silver. In 1934 she lost 211 million ounces. In the spring of 1935 China imposed the death penalty on smugglers, but she lost 218 million ounces that year, 219 million in 1936, 300 million in 1937. On November 3, 1935 (a Sunday), Dr. Kung announced the currency reform, making government banknotes legal tender, discharging debts of silver obligation, requiring holders of silver to trade it in for banknotes, establishing a Central Bank. This set the stage for unlimited inflation, creating the financial chaos which the Communists found so useful. But at the time most foreign governments thought the Chinese monetary "reform" was good. The one great exception was Japan, which interpreted these events as an attempt by Britain to extend British influence in the Orient. Japan attacked North China in July 1937 and Shanghai in August.

China was not the only nation to suffer damage by our silver policy. Mexico had a silver peso that contained a peso's worth of silver bullion whenever the price of silver hit 71.9¢ an ounce (monetary people would say: the *bullion parity* of the Mexican peso was 71.9¢). When Roosevelt raised the Treasury's buying price to 77.57¢ on April 10, 1935, the Mexican peso was endangered. The Mexican Finance Minister, Eduardo Suarez, flew to Washington on April 28 (a Sunday) to confer with Treasury Secretary Morgenthau. On April 29 Morgenthau and Suarez announced that all would be well. Nevertheless the Mexican banks opened that day issuing bronze coins to replace silver, and on May 24 Mexico decreed a reduction in the silver content of new coins.

And the damage did not stop with China and Mexico. Other countries had to call in their silver coins, prohibit melting or export, and issue new currency of paper or debased metal. Such were Peru, Costa Rica, Guatemala, Colombia, Ecuador, Uruguay, El Salvador, Bolivia. On May 14 the Italian government prohibited the export of silver even in the form of jewelry; her bullion parity had not been reached, but she was in need of silver for the large quantities of Maria Theresa dollars she was coining for use in Ethiopia (using, it was reported, an official die bought from the Vienna mint).

Very little silver coinage occurred in the world of 1934 and 1935. Foreign treasurers were shy of a metal so subject to U.S. political influence. The silver policy of the Roosevelt Administration wrecked the monetary system of China, tumbled the coinages of a half dozen other countries, disrupted the silver market for two years, and failed to achieve even its nominal purpose. It had been the published goal to raise the ratio of silver to gold in the Treasury holdings to one-third. But between 1934 and 1942 a vast flow occurred of gold towards America, as private fortunes sought to escape the foreseeable ravages of Nazism and war. The silver ratio in Treasury reserves never approached the goal set in the Silver Purchase Act, and in fact was lower in 1941 than it had been in 1934. Meanwhile the Treasury had bought 2,596,300,000 ounces of silver at a cost of almost $1.4 billion.

Against this vast hoard of silver purchased, the Treasury issued silver certificates (the familiar, but moribund, $1, $5, and $10 bills), but only to the amount of the cost of the silver purchased. For every ounce of silver the Treasury could issue $1.29+ worth of silver certificates: that is the "monetary value" or "coining value" of silver—practically unchanged since the recommendation by Alexander Hamilton. But the Treasury paid, on average, about 64¢ an ounce for the silver it bought. Therefore fully half of the silver it acquired was not needed for "backing" of the paper bills issued, and went into the Treasury's general fund. This so-called "free silver" reached its maximum level on May 6, 1942, when it totaled 1,365,468,438 ounces. Until then it had been used mainly for subsidiary coinage. During the second World War 410 million ounces were loaned to our allies, and some 900 million ounces were loaned to U.S. defense industries. The loans have been repaid. In 1943 the Congress authorized the sale of free silver to U.S. industry at 71.11¢ an ounce. In 1946 (Act of July 31, 1946) the Congress raised that offering price to 90.5¢ an ounce.

The 1946 Act also raised to 90.5¢ the price the Treasury must pay for purchases of silver. This was the last gasp of the silver bloc. Not long thereafter the market began to run away with the situation.

But in 1946 all seemed well. After the terrific storms of the 1880s and 1890s, after the subsidies, the mintings, the meltings, the purchases at artificial prices and sales at artificial prices, the confusion of the 1930s, the destruction of China's monetary system, the acquisition of the world's largest stockpile, the lucky discovery that the stockpile was useful in war—after all this, in 1946 the outlook appeared halcyon indeed. There were about two billion ounces backing up the silver certificates and no one was redeeming the certificates. The huge supply of free silver was entirely sufficient for subsidiary coinage and the foreseeable needs of industry. The price of 90.5¢, which the Treasury by law was required to pay for silver and receive for silver, was not terribly out of line with the world market. The Treasury held about 360 million silver dollars with a bullion parity of $1.29—and surely silver would never rise to *that* price! Subsidiary silver coin was being minted at $1.38—higher still, and of course entirely out of danger. The folly of the Roosevelt years was a thing of the past. International monetary cooperation was the hope of the future. All seemed well. There was nothing to fear on the monetary front. Only the most determined pessimist would have thought a storm was brewing.

4.   The Treasury Muffs the Challenge

ONE OF THE MOST incredible things about the present silver snarl is that it appears to have taken the Treasury by surprise. The story of the Government's bureaucratic bungling is entertaining but is hardly unique in a system that has bungled many a program. The Treasury must stand indicted of failure on two counts. It failed to understand the meaning of a half-dozen early warnings of the impending troubles in the silver market and in the U.S. silver coinage. And, once the problem was unavoidably in evidence, the Treasury failed to understand the urgency of it and failed to react with appropriate measures. This indictment is, I believe, amply supported by the actual record.

One of the earliest indications of something new in the air was the action of the market price for silver after the second World War. It came down off the immediate postwar high but it refused to settle at anywhere near the old price of 40¢ to 60¢ which had prevailed since 1920. The average price at which silver traded in New York was 71.8¢ in 1947, 74.4¢ in 1948, 71.9¢ in 1949, 74.2¢ in 1950, 89.4¢ in 1951 (perilously close to the Treasury's fixed price of 90.5¢), 84.9¢ in 1952, 85.2¢ in 1953, 85.2¢ in 1954, 89.1¢ in 1955.

...No doubt the Treasury thought that if the price of silver went up too far, the Congress would accommodate the Treasury by raising the Treasury's pegged price to conform more or less with the market. The unasked question was: what happens if silver hits the bullion parity of $1.29? Considering the billions of dollars involved in the silver coinage and the Treasury reserves, it was the kind of question a prudent governor should have asked. And it was not out of the range of ordinary expectation that silver might go up still further—indeed, considering the inelasticity of supply, the presumption was stronger than ever. Between 1946 and 1958, for example, the price of copper rose 150 per cent, lead 125 per cent, aluminum and zinc and tin 100 per cent. Yet silver had risen only 30 per cent. Another 50 per cent rise in silver would threaten the coinage. This much a prudent manager might have known in 1958; a very prudent manager might have thought to allow for the contingency as early as 1954 or 1955. The April 4, 1955, issue of *Barron's* magazine carried an article by John Chamberlain outlining the new industrial uses of silver and discussing the possibility of its demonetization. As far as is known, the Treasury knew nothing and did nothing.

A second indication that times had changed was the way silver dollars were acting. They had never been a coin for popular circulation. The Treasury had always held the great bulk of them. Even in the political heyday of silver, around the turn of the century, the Treasury held several hundred million silver dollars and only 66 million silver dollars were in the hands of the public. The public had never held more than a hundred million silver dollars in its own hands until 1945. After that the outflow accelerated. In 1950 the public held 170 million silver dollars. In 1956, for the first time since the dollar arbitrage of 1806, there were more silver dollars in the hands of the public than there were in the Treasury and Federal Reserve banks. The question might reasonably have been asked in 1956: Why is this happening? Why, for the first time in a century and a half, is this large silver coin flowing into the public's pockets? Who is taking these and where are they going? As far as is known, the questions were not asked.

A third indication, and an extremely strong one, also appeared in 1956, along with the puzzling outflow of silver dollars. *In 1956, for the first time in a period of general peace, Free World consumption of silver for industry and arts alone exceeded Free World production of silver.*[1] That event should have caused serious concern among the monetary managers of the Free World. If, upon investigation, they found that the deficit was traceable to an extraordinary and seemingly irreversible growth in the industrial consumption of silver, then it was perfectly obvious at that time that the Free World would sooner or later exhaust its reserves of silver for coinage purposes. I find no hint in the literature that anyone in authority suspected that something important was happening in the pattern of silver consumption. The Treasury apparently knew nothing. Certainly it did nothing. To this day the statistics on silver are reported in such a way as to hide the underlying shifts in the structure of the market. In 1956 any statistician could have ascertained that the world consumption of silver in industry and the arts had grown by 32 per cent in the preceding five years while world production of silver had stood still, and that there was now a deficit on industry and art account alone, not to mention the coinage requirements.

A fourth indication of possible trouble was the rise of the

world price of silver to slightly above the Treasury's "fix" in 1959—an event foreseen by John Chamberlain in his 1955 article. In 1959 the London silver market fluctuated between 92¢ and 94¢, just enough above the Treasury's 90.5¢ to divert to London some silver shipments that would ordinarily have found their way to New York. This rise in the market price of silver to a point above the Treasury "fix" should have confirmed the suspicions that might have been awakened by the appearance of the silver deficit in 1956. From now on the Treasury could count on being asked to make its silver available to the world market at the fixed and artificially low price of 90.5¢. Was there enough silver in the Treasury to subsidize the market both foreign and domestic? There is no record that the question was asked. If it was asked, there is no record that anyone at the Treasury understood the need for concern.

A fifth indication of the fundamental shift in the silver market occurred also in 1959. For the first time since the price had been pegged at 90.5¢, the Treasury was a net seller of silver from its free reserves. The Treasury had bought 40.0 million ounces in 1957 and 74.8 million ounces in 1958. But in 1959 the rise in the world market left the Treasury behind, and customers began to appear, asking for the cheap silver. In 1959 the Treasury sold 27.1 million ounces, net. That should have been a loud signal. Apparently it went unheard in the halls of the mighty. It was confirmed, more loudly than before, in 1960 when the Treasury's net sales of silver climbed to 51.6 million ounces. It was blared out fortissimo in 1961 when the Treasury sold 95.1 million ounces, taking its free reserves down almost to zero. Finally some action was taken, after the emergency had blown up in full force. That action I shall describe later. Here I am focusing on the warning signals that went unheeded. In the case of the diminishing reserves, the Treasury apparently knew nothing. Certainly it did nothing—until it was too late.

A sixth indication was available also in 1959. This was the tapering off of the return flow of silver from our wartime allies. We had loaned them 410 million ounces to facilitate their military production lines. They had returned two-thirds of that sum by the end of 1957. They paid back 103.4 million ounces in 1958, and 45.0 million ounces in 1959. After that, there was very little silver to look to from that source. It was perfectly predictable. It was according to contract. One major source was drying up. The Treasury knew nothing, or if it knew then it did not care. In any case it did nothing.

The emergency that was upon us in the spring of 1965 could have been predicted, then, as much as nine or ten years earlier. Certainly there is no question that it could have been predicted six years earlier. I may be accused of using the always 20-20 hindsight when I accuse the Treasury of failing to read the warning signals properly in 1955 or 1956. But the case against the Treasury grows to undeniably damning proportions when the year 1959 is reached. For in the year 1959 at least one voice was raised in alarm. The late Mr. J. B. Lynch, President of Siscoe Metals of Ontario, Canada, began in 1959 a campaign to warn Washington of the onrushing disaster in silver.[2] He "repeatedly" tried to explain the gravity of the problem to Treasury officials and to certain members of Congress in yearly visits starting in 1959 and in correspondence. Either official Washington was incapable of understanding the situation, or it consciously chose to get rid of silver in the most awkward manner possible.

Indeed, the lethargy of the Treasury approaches sleeping sickness. Coin shortages had been reported as early as 1959, particularly by some banks in Baltimore. Correspondence between the Mint and the Federal Reserve System in 1960 and again in 1961 touched upon the then existing coin shortages. In July 1960 the Federal Reserve Board wrote to the Treasury about the coin shortage, and the Treasury replied with a long and complacent review of its actions, concluding, "We assure you that we are doing everything in our power to relieve the present situation as rapidly as possible and to provide for the future." In August 1961 the FRB again wrote to the Treasury, mentioning the sporadic coin shortages of the past ten (!) years, and offering to cooperate in a new and different system for predicting the nation's coin needs. The Treasury rejected the suggestion. In November 1962 the FRB wrote to the Treasury again, in anticipation of a severe coin shortage during the Christmas season, "with the hope that some emergency measures may be possible to ease the current shortage of coins and avoid a recurrence of this situation in the future." Three weeks later, Treasury Secretary Dillon replied that funds would be needed to increase coin production at the Mint, and ended with the light-hearted note that "I look forward hopefully to the millennium when the inventories of coin in the mints and the Federal Reserve banks will be adequate to weather peak demands." In January 1964 the FRB once again wrote to the Treasury, commenting that the coin shortage was worse than ever. Two weeks later the Treasury replied that all would be well if it could only produce more coins, "given sufficient funds," and ultimately "given" a new mint or two. In mid-1964 the Treasury finally announced a "crash" program of minting; and it seems to have been goaded into that action only by the announcement that a House subcommittee would start hearings on the coinage situation.[3]

In 1961 the Treasury, making good on its offer of silver at 90.5¢ an ounce, went through 75 per cent of its free reserves of silver. That was the shock that awakened official Washington. Suddenly the managers of the nation's destinies noticed that half of all the silver being used in U.S. industry was coming from Treasury stocks—at below-market prices. On October 9 the first faint stirrings of reaction to the emergency could be detected: on that day the silver situation was administratively transferred from the Bureau of the Mint to a new office in the Treasury. It was to be called the Office of Domestic Gold and Silver Operations. It was placed directly under the supervision of Robert V. Roosa, Under Secretary of the Treasury, who was in charge (if that is not too strong a phrase) of monetary affairs. Mr. Roosa appears to have done nothing. After several years he resigned, late in 1964, to return to the world of business.

After creating the Office of Domestic Gold and Silver Operations, the Kennedy Administration subsided into coma once again. It was awakened shortly by the incredible acceleration of silver sales from the Treasury. On November 28, 1961, President Kennedy directed Treasury Secretary Douglas Dillon to stop selling free silver. The price rose immediately to more than $1.00 an ounce. Mr. Simon D. Strauss, Vice President of American Smelting & Refining, announced with a reassuring yawn that if the price reached $1.10 a great deal of silver would come out of hiding, and exploration and production would be encouraged.[4]

Also on November 28, 1961, President Kennedy directed the Treasury to reduce the circulation of silver certificates in order to liberate some of the silver bullion that was backing those bills. The Treasury announced, with some pride and expertise, that it had had the silver situation "under study for some time."[5] Its intention was to withdraw silver certificates over a period of 30 years.[6] In practice they went ten times as fast.

Also in late 1961 the Department of the Interior increased its efforts to find new silver deposits. It greatly raised the proportion it would pay of the expenses of new explorations. Since then it has underwritten the lion's share of the costs of 16 exploratory ventures, four of which have disbanded for lack of luck, and 12 of which are still nosing around. Nothing has been found to date.

Now there was a veritable chorus of experts. Everyone agreed that there was (ho-hum) nothing to worry about. The December 1961 issue of the First National City Bank *Monthly Letter* was positively fatherly in its tone of reassurance: "Few practical observers expect that the price of silver will rise to anything like $1.29 [it did just that within 19 months], particularly since the Treasury will take care of its requirements for subsidiary silver coinage by retiring silver certificates [irrelevant: the problem was industrial demand, not subsidiary silver coinage]....With all our silver treasure, there is no need to follow the example of some other countries which have totally demonetized silver and swung over to cheaper metals for all coins. We can afford to keep silver in subsidiary coinage." [We didn't.] Well, "all our silver treasure" stood at 1,862.3 million ounces in December 1961. Three years later it was down to 1,218.0 million ounces, and draining faster than ever. By year-end 1965 it was near 800 million ounces. The bottom of the barrel was within view.

In February 1962 the President asked the Congress for

legislation to repeal all the existing silver purchase legislation, specifically including the 50% tax on gains from trans-
fers of interest in bullion. Bills were drawn up and submitted
to the two Committees on Banking and Currency. Nothing
came of it. The Congress, too, was apathetic.

The price of $1.29 and the inaction of the Congress de-
serve some remark. By law the silver dollar contains approximately 0.77 of an ounce of silver. When the market price of
silver hits $1.29, there is just about a dollar's worth of metal
in the silver dollar. That is why, late in 1963, when the market price of silver had reached $1.29, the Treasury had to
resume sales of silver to industrial users in an attempt to
hold the price down to $1.29. If the price were allowed to
rise above that, every silver dollar would disappear, either
to be hoarded or to be melted down.

As to the inactivity of the Congress on this monetary
matter, there may have been some reason to ignore, early in
1962, the situation arising under one of the categories of
powers that the Constitutional Convention thought so important that it enumerated 17 of them as specific powers of
the Congress: "To coin money, regulate the value thereof...."
The reason seems to have been that the Administration itself
did not understand the nature of the forces working against
the Treasury. The 1961 buying of silver had been, in large
part, speculative—either for speculative buildup of inventories destined eventually for industrial use, or for genuine
speculative holding in traders' hands. The Administration,
understandably reluctant to serve as the target for silver
speculators, undoubtedly approached the Congress with an
appeal to reinstitute a free market in silver so that the buyers
and sellers, the hagglers and gamblers, the merchants and
miners, could work things out amongst themselves, not shak-

ing the dignity of the Treasury, and incidentally calling new production into being through a rise in the market price. The Congress would not have seen the urgency of repealing all the silver statutes simply because of a temporary and speculative fluctuation in the market. So it did nothing. And it was in good company. The First National City Bank *Monthly Letter* for December 1962 echoed the placid tones it had used a year earlier. "It might be said that there is no particular urgency in considering these proposals—if only because there are some 382 million ounces of silver that can, without new legislation, be made available for coinage. . . . People rarely do want silver dollars [within 15 months they had sacked the Treasury of its silver dollars]. . . . A workable and efficient silver market is needed to do the job of equating supply and demand." (Treasury stocks declined by 365 million ounces in 1964; people *do* want silver dollars; and as to equating supply and demand, repeat a hundred times: Silver is a by-product. . . .)

In the spring of 1963, Treasury Secretary Dillon testified that the nation had enough silver for its coinage needs until the 1980s.[7]

When the passage of time brought nothing but deterioration in the Treasury's silver position, Congress took action. On June 4, 1963, Public Law 88-36 became effective. It repealed the Silver Purchase Act of 1934, the Act of July 6, 1939, and the Act of July 31, 1946. The 1963 Act recognized the President's request (of November 1961 and February 1962) for authority to issue $1 Federal Reserve Notes. The new act also abolished the special tax on silver dealings, clearing the way for a free market in silver for the first time in 30 years. Finally, the new act confirmed the redeemability of silver certificates in commercial bar form.

Silver dealings on the New York Commodity Exchange were resumed on June 12, 1963, for the first time since August 9, 1934. By July 5, one-year futures contracts were trading at 131.35¢—above the melting point for silver dollars. Consequently Douglas Dillon, Secretary of the Treasury, published on July 23 a letter (dated July 22) of instructions, telling the world how to lay its hands on Treasury silver without paying a premium (which is undignified, because it amounts to someone other than Secretary Dillon undercutting the coin). Just deposit your funds with the United States Assay Office either in New York or in San Francisco, urged the Secretary—they needn't be silver certificates—and attach a letter stating your intention to withdraw silver bullion. The Federal Reserve will then proceed to collect silver certificates equal in amount to the funds you have deposited. It will effect the switch on the books; and you can walk off with your silver bullion. The effect of Dillon's letter was to depress the futures prices, temporarily. Within a few months they rose to about 137¢, pretty close to the melting point for subsidiary silver coins.

Said the *Wall Street Journal* in September 1963: "Some industry officials believe the Government should cut the silver in coins if there is a continuing heavy drain on U.S. Treasury stocks."

Now as all this was going on, there was also developing another problem, the exquisite final straw for the camel's back. Simultaneously with the departure and disappearance of the silver dollar, a shortage was developing in subsidiary silver coin (halves, quarters, dimes). The cause of the shortage was, as far as the Administration was concerned, numismatists, speculators, and vending machines. Time and again it was pointed out that the number of coin hobbyists had grown from two million to eight million in the past decade. The thought of speculating against the Treasury's vast hoard of silver was, it was announced, ridiculous. (Similar ridicule was aimed at gold speculators in January 1965; it is always a bad sign.) And vending machines were, it was said, gobbling up the coin. I have dealt with these arguments earlier.

The official Washington response to this gathering mess in the currency was to continue as before, only more so. Minting was stepped up. In 1958 the Treasury had used 38.2 million ounces of silver in coinage. That figure climbed steeply to 41.4 million in 1959, 46.0 million in 1960, 55.9 million in 1961, 77.4 million in 1962, 111.3 million in 1963, and 203.0 million in 1964! It was about 300 million ounces in 1965! The Treasury apparently believed that there was simply a shortage of coin, and that a larger supply would satisfy everyone. It acted as if it had never heard of Gresham's Law.

The mints produced 1.5 billion pieces in 1959, 3 billion in 1963, and 4.3 billion in 1964. The 1965 production was approximately 9 billion pieces. There are now about 50 billion pieces outstanding. Normal replacement and population growth impose a minting requirement of about 2 billion pieces a year. It was hard to see how the plans to mint more coins (of the old silver content) would have any effect on the problem. One can only sympathize with the uninformed, such as the consulting firm of Arthur D. Little Inc., which submitted a report to the Congress early in 1963 entitled *Additional Mint Facilities*, in which it was declared that "the recent rapid increase in coin demand seems to be nothing more than a catching up (with possibly some overshoot) after the 1958 recession."

In the stately mime of Washington activity, 1961 was the

year in which the silver "problem" came to official notice. In 1962 the Executive asked the Congress to pass laws creating a free silver market. In 1963 Congress did so. In 1964 the "problem" became a full-fledged emergency.

The year 1964 started with a bang. In the January budget message, the Treasury made the incredible request for funds to produce 50 million new silver dollars before June 30 and 100 million new silver dollars in fiscal 1965. (It had lost 61 million silver dollars in 1963 alone.) The House Appropriations Committee wisely refused funds to the Treasury for minting new silver dollars, but its reasoning was less than satisfactory: it admonished the Treasury that the effort should be concentrated on stepping up production of minor coin at the Denver and Philadelphia mints, and it granted the Treasury additional funds for that purpose.

Crowds of people were laying siege to the Treasury Building in Washington, asking for silver dollars. Treasury officials called it the "nonsense" of coin collecting. Spokesmen laughed, saying all the silver dollars would be back in the Treasury vaults before long. Secretary Dillon threatened indirectly to start giving silver pellets rather than silver dollars in return for silver certificates. The headline in mid-March said: "Treasury Sets Defenses Against Collectors...."[8] By the end of March the Treasury was down to its last three million silver dollars, and Secretary Dillon announced (March 25) that the Treasury would no longer redeem silver certificates in silver dollars. Instead, holders of silver certificates would be given packets of silver pellets in the case of small redemptions, and standard 1,000-ounce silver bars for larger transactions. Secretary Dillon explained that the final three million silver dollars could not be handed out, because they might end up in the hands of "collectors." Once again the stereotype of the collector haunts the Treasury; and, if those last three million coins are genuine collector's items, how to explain that the preceding 482 million silver dollars, now in the hands of the public, have disappeared from general circulation? Is *every* silver dollar a thing of value? (Yes.) Will every silver coin become a thing of value, as things are going these days? (Yes.)

At this same time (March, 1964) the Treasury made available the first half-dollar pieces bearing the image of the late President Kennedy. In view of the worsening situation in silver the production of this new coin, which was destined to enjoy a huge popularity, was a sign of unspeakably bad judgment. In any case, the long lines were waiting in March 1964 for the Kennedy halves. The Treasury had originally planned to mint 90 million of them. They were minted, and they disappeared from circulation. The target was raised to 150 million Kennedy halves. By July 1964 the Treasury was talking about 200 million Kennedy halves. That would be one per person. Assistant Secretary of the Treasury Robert A. Wallace said in July 1964: "We'll just keep on making them until there are enough."[9] By February 1965 more than 235 million Kennedy halves had been minted, and still they were withheld from circulation. Once again the Treasury seemed to consider it only a supply problem: give the people enough coins and all will be well. The thought had not seeped through, yet, that the people might be preferring hard silver to soft paper. . . . Four months later the President solemnly authorized the minting of 45 million silver dollars—an action which was widely and correctly interpreted at the time as the crudest form of bluff. The coins, of course, were never minted. By year-end 1965 almost 400 million of the original 90-per-cent-silver Kennedy halves had been minted, but they still refused to enter into general circulation.

On March 30, 1964, the Senate first formally considered

reducing the silver content of the coinage. Nothing came of the movement at that time, at least in terms of law written and passed; but the publicity had its effect. By early April there were articles in the newspapers about "coin shortages" in the United States. In one article (*New York Times,* April 5) the chairman of the Federal Reserve Board, William McChesney Martin, was quoted as saying: "There is a chronic, serious coin shortage in this country." And in the same article Mr. Robert A. Wallace (whom we have met before, and shall meet again) said: "Between now and three years from now, the earliest a new Philadelphia mint could be put in opera- tion, we're going to have some very difficult times." *Barron's* magazine, April 27, 1964, estimated that at the then rate of silver consumption, the Treasury would run out of silver "before the end of the decade." Robert Roosa told Congress that the Treasury had enough silver to take care of coinage until 1972. (He resigned.)

By May 1964 the *Wall Street Journal* was carrying adver- tisements placed by small firms in Nevada who purported to offer valuable poundages of "vanishing silver dollars" for a 50 per cent markup.

On May 7 the Bureau of the Mint announced that it had stopped accepting orders for sets of uncirculated coins of 1964. The uncirculated sets, known also as mint sets, con- tained ten coins each (two each of the penny, nickel, dime, quarter, half) with a total face value of $1.82 and a sale price of $2.40 to cover handling costs, postage, and insurance. And was it because hundreds of millions of coins were being wasted in mint sets? The Mint explained that it had received a million orders for mint sets—as against 600,000 in 1963 and something in the area of 200,000 to 300,000 in previous years. Which is to say that the demand for mint sets soaked up about one-fifth of one per cent of the pieces struck in 1963:

hardly a clear and present danger to the coinage. But one must always remember that the Treasury and the Administration were at war against the spectral "collector" and the "numismatist."

In June 1964 the Senate Appropriations Committee approved funds for the minting of 45 million silver dollars—although the House had turned down a Treasury request in January (noted above) for funds to mint 150 million silver dollars. Perhaps more than one observer wondered to himself at the time if this new development wasn't merely a piece of bravado on the part of an almost bankrupt government: offering to mint new silver dollars when there wasn't enough silver to handle the current requirements, hoping to bluff the hoarders into dishoarding. In June 1964 the silver stock of the Treasury declined by 19.4 million ounces. *Nothing* seemed to work!

At the end of June the Treasury announced two new steps to "fight" those old bogeymen, the "collectors." It would greatly expand its production of minor coin. And it would continue to use the date 1964 on coins minted after the close of 1964. The Treasury was apparently still operating under the assumption that people were collecting names and dates, rather than solid silver that they thought might be a store of value in the future, and a more reliable store of value than bits of paper or the promises of politicians.

At this time, also, the Treasury announced that it would fill its present orders for a million proof sets and cease, forthwith, supplying such sets to the fraternity of "collectors"—the old villains. Assistant Secretary Wallace was quoted in the June 29 *Wall Street Journal* as saying that the plans for stepped-up production of coins "will alleviate the coin shortage this fall and end it altogether next year." *Poor* Mr. Wallace!

Early in July the Treasury announced that it expected the

increased minting of Kennedy halves to end the black market. Assistant Treasury Secretary Robert Wallace said that if people would "just be patient," then they'd have their fill of "literally billions" of Kennedy halves.[9] (At the time of that statement, the Treasury reserves of silver, if applied exclusively to the production of Kennedy halves, would have accommodated the production of about 3.5 billion pieces; it would have been ironic if Kennedy's graven image had broken the United States Treasury.) The presumption is that when Mr. Wallace said "literally," he was not being literal.

On July 1, Federal Reserve Board Chairman William M. Martin told the House Monetary Affairs Subcommittee that the only way to end the coin shortage was to flood the market with coin. "This would remove the incentive to hold on to excess coin," said the chairman of the FRB and the most recent convert to the theory that silver is more worthless than paper. Mr. Martin also gave his support to the Treasury proposal to keep the 1964 minting date on coins minted after the end of the year 1964—as a sally against "collectors and speculators," as Mr. Martin termed the enemy.[10]

By mid-July 1964 the gross markup on silver dollars in quantity had reached 20 per cent.

At the end of July the Congress sent to the President (who signed it early in August) an appropriations bill that included authority for the Treasury to mint 45 million new silver dollars. In view of the rapidly declining Treasury reserves of silver, the appropriation could hardly be believed on the surface. Especially in view of the history of the Treasury request since January, the presumption gains force that the Treasury wanted this authorization only as a bit of psychological warfare in its death struggle with "collectors and speculators." That is, if the Treasury could make a believable pretense even to thinking of minting 45 million new silver dollars, the first since 1935, out of a silver reserve that was half what it was at the beginning of the Second World War—why then, everything was in good shape, what?

United States coinage needs alone by mid-year 1964 were running at a rate that was equal to the entire Free World output of newly mined silver.

In July 1964 the Treasury silver stock declined by 21.7 million ounces.

Assistant Secretary Wallace said at this time that the coin shortage wasn't terribly serious: "I will say that this fall the situation is likely to be tight, but I do not look for a crisis. I think our program to double coin production will end the shortage early next year."[9] (Earlier in the year poor Mr. Wallace had foreseen "very difficult times" into the spring of 1967; by mid-year he foresaw that the new production would "alleviate the coin shortage this fall.") Mr. Wallace, testifying before the Senate Banking Committee, blamed commercial hoarders and numismatists for the coin shortage.

On August 3 the "war against coin collectors" got a new shot in the arm when Currency Comptroller James J. Saxon curtailed the ability of national banks under his control to make loans for which coin collections are collateral. It appears that some coin speculators had actually been offering United States silver money as collateral for bank loans, and the Currency Comptroller (an insider) would not allow such shenanigans. In the past, banks had been allowing up to 100 per cent of face value of coins as collateral for loans. Mr. Saxon cut that down to 70 per cent.

On August 11 the Treasury let it be known that it was going to put an 86-year-old coin press back into service: the press that was built in Carson City in 1878 and was used to turn out the famous Carson City Dollars, beloved of collectors. The coin press had been in a museum in Carson City since 1955, but it would serve its purpose: not necessarily high-speed production, but certainly high-potency propaganda. If the Treasury was going to mint Carson City Dollars, the finest of the recently fine, then what was left for us poor collectors? The announcement, which was backed by no serious intention at all on the part of the Treasury, fell through immediately. Silver dollars remained silver dollars, and they remained in the pockets of the "collectors." On the same day Mr. Assistant Secretary Wallace said: "There's no question but what the shortage will be over early next year."[11] And it began to look as if poor Mr. Wallace had been hired to do the lying that Secretary Dillon felt might be beneath him. Wallace placed the blame for the coin shortage on businessmen hoarders, private hoarders and speculators, and vending machines (give him a C minus). When asked where the shortage is most serious, Wallace said categorically: "In pennies and nickels in particular." (But pennies and nickels don't take so much silver: where's the silver going? And if pennies and nickels are indeed scarce, which Mr. Wallace's solemn assurance by no means guarantees, why ask for funds to increase production of silver dollars and Kennedy halves, and why bite into the silver reserve so heavily for production of new quarters and dimes?—But Mr. Wallace remains an inscrutable contradiction.)

Late in August 1964 the Congress approved and sent to the President a bill authorizing the 1964 date to be kept on coins minted in 1965 and later—in order to discourage "hoarding and collecting," as one news story put it. At the same time the Federal Reserve Bank of New York announced that it was using old and new coins together when filling orders for coin from commercial banks—in order to discourage speculative hoarding. The Treasury silver stock declined in August by 24.0 million ounces.

On September 15, 1964, the Secretary of the Interior, Stewart Udall, announced that the Bureau of Mines had completed a special study, having been informed that there were some questions about the longer-term availability of silver, and as a result of that study the Department of the Interior would raise its subsidy of silver exploration costs from the present 50 per cent to a new level of 75 per cent.[12] Mr. Udall, obviously excited at the news that something had been happening in silver, announced that he had mobilized the entire Department on a crash basis. Crash! Bam! Zowie! The Office of Minerals Exploration would explore for silver. Crash! The Office of Minerals and Solid Fuels would look into the need for silver in a future hypothetical war. Bam! The Geological Survey would forthwith march double-time to Nevada and produce a survey outlining the areas that might have silver near the surface. Zowie! Mr. Udall directed the Bureau of Mines to give special emphasis to "mining and metallurgical research and also in its nationwide resource evaluation investigations"—a directive that must have been not too unsettling to the silver speculators. "Developments are being watched closely," said Mr. Udall, in a phrase that bore all the hallmarks of the sterling bureaucrat. Three years earlier, the Treasury had announced that it had had the silver problem under close study for some time. . . . But it must be noted that Mr. Udall's report *did* mention that silver is generally mined as a by-product, and therefore cannot be expected to respond too directly to rises in the market price. Mr. Udall deserves our respect for that, at least. In September the Treasury silver stock declined by 41.9 million ounces.

Early in October 1964 poor Mr. Assistant Secretary Robert Wallace denied rumors that the Treasury had any plans to reduce or eliminate the silver content in the coinage.[13] A great multitude of possibilities were being considered, said he, and in any case the Treasury had enough silver on hand to take care of coinage needs for the next seven years. *The next seven years*. Simultaneously, the Treasury Department's Bureau of the Mint announced another great weapon in the battle against the hated collector: from then on the monthly production reports from Philadelphia and Denver would be consolidated, so that collectors would have no way of knowing the separate production figures per coin per mint per month. The news article languidly commented that "thus a favorite form of profiteering is eliminated." It is difficult to understand how a discrepancy between the monthly production runs of pennies in Denver and Philadelphia could lead to the disappearance of the United States coinage, but apparently the Bureau of the Mint was satisfied that this new step would help to solve the problem of the coin shortage. In October, too, the first outright admission of defeat on the part of official Washington became obvious.[14] The Treasury Department "in cooperation with" local banks around the country began to issue advertisements on radio and television, urging the general public to stop saving coins, to take their coins to their friendly local banks, and to turn them in and get good paper dollars for them, in order to help their Government out of a temporary difficulty. One wonders: if the numismatist is really the culprit, why beg coins on television instead of in the pages of the numismatic journals? Or if speculators are the villain, is it possible that the whole country had begun to speculate against the coinage? (It is possible; but it's not necessary for the whole country to do it, in order to make a television appeal worth while.) And also, a normal reaction to such appeals would be to clutch the coinage tighter. "I've got it, and he wants it, eh? I'm not selling until I hear his price." Secretary Dillon (who resigned in March 1965) placed the blame squarely on speculators. He asked the American Bankers Association to help broadcast anti-piggy-bank commercials on 600 television stations and 4,000 radio stations. It is at least arguable that the advertising campaign had an unforeseen effect: it merely convinced people of the importance of holding their silver. Late in October Dr. Vladimir Clain-Stefanelli, Curator of Numismatics at the Smithsonian Institution, addressing the American Society of Metals in Philadelphia, called for the total abandonment of silver in the United States coinage.[15] By mid-October 137 million Kennedy halves had been minted and had disappeared. During the month of October the Treasury's silver stock declined by 65.9 million ounces.

An interpretive news article in the *New York Herald Tribune*, dated December 6, 1964, and carrying somewhat more of the air of authority than that paper's articles normally exhibit, implied that the Treasury report on the currency, which was expected in February or March of 1965, would urge a great reduction of the silver content in the coinage. The article mentioned also that the Treasury was thinking of calling in silver coins, just as it had called in gold coins a generation ago. Big question: would President Johnson make it a crime to own a Kennedy half-dollar?

By mid-December 1964 it was reported that a private research institute, the Battelle Memorial Institute in Columbus, Ohio, had been hired by the Treasury to take a quick, studious, but quiet look at the metals market, and see if there wasn't something that was just as good as silver but wasn't silver and wasn't gold.[16] And poor Mr. Robert Wallace was talking again: *Look* reported (December 29) that "Robert Wallace, Assistant Secretary of the Treasury, predicts that our chicken-feed problems will be almost over by next fall." (That's the fall of 1965.) By the end of December it was reported that the Federal Reserve Bank of New York was issuing coins to commercial banks on a quota basis; that most of the commercial banks' customers had to get along with 40 per cent of their normal allotment of coin; and that an official of the Chase Manhattan Bank was "amazed . . . that they [the Treasury officials] have been working so hard and so long and there has not even been a drop in the bucket of improvement in the situation." On the 28th of December it was announced that the Treasury would not, after all, produce the 45 million new silver dollars for which it had received Congressional and Presidential approval in July and August. During the year 1964 the Treasury silver stock declined by 23 per cent.

In January 1965 the publicity campaign that Secretary Dillon had kicked off in October was taking hold. Depositors in major commercial banks around the country began receiving notices in their monthly statements, explaining that the Treasury was terribly short of cash, and that it was almost the patriotic duty of every citizen to turn in his money and get good spanking new dollar bills in return. The mining industry, rather than see the entire market go down the drain, announced that it would be satisfied with a reduction of the silver content in the coinage, rather than outright elimination of silver. President Johnson in mid-January 1965 asked Congress to repeal the law requiring gold backing for the deposits of commercial banks in the Federal Reserve banking system.

The Treasury report that had been due in February and

postponed to April was postponed again. Douglas Dillon resigned. The new Treasury Secretary, Mr. Henry Fowler, rejected the first copy of the report.[17] In mid-May 1965 the silver still flowed out of the Treasury like blood from an open artery, and there was no indication that anyone knew what to do or that anyone was in fact working very seriously at the problem.

The record of official Washington is indescribably inept in this case. The Treasury in particular is guilty. What its 88,000 employees have been doing to earn their keep, no one knows. The Treasury failed to detect the new trends, although the signs were multiplying after 1955. It failed to act on the information given it voluntarily by people such as Mr. Lynch, in 1959 and afterwards. It had to lose three-quarters of its free reserves before it awoke to the existence of an abnormality. Its immediate action was based on a faulty interpretation of the circumstances (first the numismatists were guilty; then the vending machines; then economic growth). Its subsequent actions were inadequate and delayed. It failed to anticipate the price rise in silver after it withdrew from supplying half of domestic industrial demand. Having announced in 1961 that it had had the problem under study, it hired in 1964 a private institute to study the problem. Every official forecast was wrong. Douglas Dillon's famous prophecy that we have enough silver to last into the 1980s, and almost any statement by poor Mr. Wallace, will serve as samples of the uninformed, haphazard, or deliberately deceptive pronouncements that have characterized the Treasury in recent years. Finally, in the face of all the evidence of a terrible silver shortage, the Treasury quadrupled the production of subsidiary silver coins although there was no indication that any of them were getting into circulation; and the minting of 400 million Kennedy halves was, under the circumstances, a close approximation to lunacy.

Perhaps, after all, the Treasury had decided to abandon silver (which, as I point out later, is not a bad idea). But if this whole episode was designed and produced at the Treasury, it still seems that the most complicated, awkward, inefficient, and self-defeating methods were chosen.

5.   Problems in Altering a Coinage

AFTER A COINAGE has circulated for some time (and through
1965 our silver coinage, remember, was almost unchanged
from 1792), it becomes an organic part of the society that
uses it. There is hardly an event or function that is not in
some way, no matter how indirectly, accommodated to the
coinage. The more successful the coinage, the deeper it drives
into the everyday life of society and the more difficult is the
problem of altering it. If the old coinage has succeeded in
serving the uncounted needs of society, then the new coinage
must be designed to be just as good. The problems lead into
a bewildering variety of situations.

There is, for example, the problem of the vending machines. The new coinage must possess a density and a degree
of electrical conductivity that will be 1) highly individual and
2) easily measured by the rejection devices in the vending
machines. And these qualities must exist in a coin that is
difficult to counterfeit. Now it happens that the operators of
vending machines adjust their machines to a narrow or broad
range of tolerance in accordance with the social mores of
the neighborhood in which the machines are placed. If it's
the kind of neighborhood where experience would suggest

that a good deal of petty larceny may go on, then the vending machine operators will set the rejection devices to a very fine tolerance, in order to protect themselves from the sad experience of giving away good merchandise in return for slugs. In other neighborhoods the machines will be set broadly enough to accept an occasional bad coin, i.e., legally underweight coin, because the vendors expect to find almost no cheating, and desire of course to maximize their sales. Now a very special case happens to be the "neighborhood" that is constituted by vessels of the United States Navy. Many of the little things subject to discretionary spending that make life pleasant on shipboard are sold through automatic vending machines. Any shipboard machinist worth half his salt can use the shop equipment he has at his fingertips to turn out the finest slugs in the world. Consequently the vending machines placed on board U.S. naval vessels are customarily adjusted to an exceptionally fine tolerance. As a final consequence, and here the Treasury comes in again, any new coinage must satisfy the exacting requirements of shipboard service amidst highly talented pranksters possessed of the world's finest metalworking machinery—or else the Treasury will have contributed to poor morale on the high seas, and the Chief of Naval Operations will be heard from.

The Treasury, in short, had good reason to delay its response. The situation was of the kind that people try to ignore in the hope that it will go away, and once the problem is taken into consideration it turns out to be so complex that no solution can avoid being either late or inadequate. At first the Treasury thought that the hobby of coin-collecting lay at the root of the coin shortage. But genuine collectors had less to do with the situation than retailers and speculators—businessmen keeping their coin for use in trade rather than turning it in to the banks, and speculators amassing coin in anticipation of profits on a rise in the price of silver. The price of silver was expected to rise because the Free World was using much more silver than it was producing. The only thing that kept the price of silver steady at $1.29 was supplies from the Treasury hoards.

The Treasury was forced to make silver available at $1.29 because silver dollars would be melted down if the price went above that, and the melting of coins is often regarded as the worst shock a monetary system can sustain; the one thing that is more unsettling is devaluation itself. Furthermore, silver being such an inelastic commodity (a rising price brings in very little new production), the presumption was that there would be no point in allowing the price of silver to exceed $1.29 while holding it below $1.38. At $1.38 it would become profitable to melt down the dimes, quarters, and halves —and then the United States would appear in the ridiculous and disastrous position of having no circulating coins except pennies and nickels.

With all of the silver coinage vanished, and with a great public protest over the difficulty of carrying on small retail trade, the U.S. would present a remarkably awkward face to the world. And that would be at the very time when the world was asking itself whether the U.S. should be trusted to use good judgment in monetary matters. European bankers, for instance, holding billions of dollar claims on the U.S. gold supply, might be tempted to take their gold rather than risk a devaluation. And the devaluation seemed likely, if the U.S. should decide to reconstruct its monetary system from the ground up, abolishing silver, issuing a new coinage, and so on. But a foreign run on our gold would wipe us out—the foreigners hold short term claims amounting to more than twice our entire gold supply. If we were stripped of our gold, not only our coinage but our entire monetary system would have to be reorganized, and there was a danger that all the foreign currencies tied to ours would share in the general turmoil. In which case, the problem of the U.S. coinage might turn into a debacle for the entire Free World.

What was to be done, then? How had other countries proceeded in similar circumstances? It was known that there had been many cases of vanishing silver coinages after the great rise in the silver price during the first World War. The bullion parity of the Philippine peso had been 97.1¢ and of the subsidiary coinage $1.036. When the market price of silver hit $1.085 in September 1917, the Philippine silver coinage was in danger. The *Manila Daily Bulletin* reported on September 18, 1917, that the situation was serious:

Where is the silver change of coin of the realm gone to? This is the question now asked in all quarters of Manila, but apparently an answer is not yet forthcoming. That silver coin is fast disappearing from circulation, every resident of Manila has been made to feel recently. Stores on the Escolta and everywhere are finding it difficult to make change, while in the markets, vendors and stall holders will not change a bill even at the expense of losing a purchase. A two-peso bill may not be changed for the asking, and even an offer of purchase will not induce a Chino storekeeper to change the smallest paper money. . . . At Clarke's refreshment emporium the management had to accept two chits from customers on account of its inability to make change. Cigar stands and establishments where the Manila public are wont to congregate, found themselves yesterday in the same predicament, while yesterday the Malabon Café had to close for the night at nine o'clock for the same reason. Certain Chinese are out buying all the silver change they can lay hands on. It was stated yesterday in certain quarters that offers of seven centavos over the peso were being offered by certain silver manipulators.

On the same day, the *Manila Times* reported:

Sunday, the effect of the hoarding of the subsidiary coins and the peso, began to be apparent on the street car lines. Meralco conductors reported from all parts of the city, particularly those districts where the cockpit crowds were to be found, an unusual amount of paper currency presented for fares. So great was this condition on some lines that the conductors ran out of change completely.

The Philippine authorities responded by issuing banknotes in small denominations—1 peso, 50 centavos, 20 centavos, and 10 centavos. They also took steps to prohibit the export of silver coins (which steps were deemed successful). They were saved, however, by the fall in the market price of silver. By October the crisis was past.

In the Straits Settlements the silver dollar had a bullion parity of 97.0¢ and the subsidiary coins $1.083. There were, also, large amounts of silver certificates in circulation. The government announced on September 7, 1917, that it would "defer" redemption of the silver certificates. Recoinage at a higher bullion parity (i.e., lower silver content) was rejected because the mints were already working at full capacity trying to handle India's coinage problems (Britain used the Indian mints for the Straits Settlements coinage). In early September the subsidiary coinage was disappearing. On September 26 the government made it a crime to keep more than a "normal" amount of subsidiary coin on hand, punishable by six months in jail and/or $850 fine. The government prohibited the export of coins except under license. A bill was passed on October 1 authorizing the issue of fractional notes— in denominations of 25 cents, 10 cents, and 5 cents. These were made legal tender for debts up to $2. Some Chinese hoarders were convicted and sentenced. The government rejected the idea of reducing the weight of the coins while maintaining the old ratio of silver. It kept the weight but reduced the silver content. In April 1918 the first coins of reduced fineness were circulated, the fineness having dropped from .600 to .400. This made a bullion parity of $1.624—substantially above the market price of silver. But the low fineness of the new coins made them unsatisfactory, and in 1926 the old .600 fineness was resumed. Also in 1926 the use of fractional notes was stopped. Specie payments had been resumed in December 1920 with a new silver dollar whose bullion parity was $2.094.

Japan went through a shortage of subsidiary silver coin in September 1917. She responded by recoining at ever higher bullion parities—from the old 95.6 cents to $1.434 in May 1918, and to $2.173 in 1922. Mexico, riled by revolutions, was using mostly paper, and the Mexican peso continued to be exported through 1920 even though Mexico raised the bullion parity from 77.4 cents to $1.068 in November 1918 and to $1.291 in October 1919. In 1919 and 1920 Siam, Ceylon, the Dutch East Indies, and French Indo-China reduced the silver content of their coins. Chile's paper-money inflation took silver past the melting point in 1921; Chile responded with a drastic cut in the silver content of the coinage.

Costa Rica took an unusual step. Silver coins were being hoarded or smuggled away because of the paper-money inflation. In 1923 the government restamped its coinage at twice the old face value; and later it recoined at that level.

Silver coins disappeared in Honduras but came back into circulation in 1920, following the great decline in the market price of silver. During the shortage, however, Honduras made U.S. money legal tender, the dollar being valued at 2 pesos. After 1920, when the Honduran peso reappeared, Honduras had two monetary standards.

In Peru, that great treasure house of silver and gold, the old silver coinage disappeared. The government was forced to issue fractional bills in denominations as small as 5 centavos. In 1921 it issued a new silver coinage at .500 fineness, replacing the old .900 fine coinage.

El Salvador in 1914 was one of the few nations still on the silver standard. Although she had silver reserves equal to 50 per cent of the note issue, she declared a moratorium on specie payments on August 11, 1914. In September 1919 she went on the gold standard, allowing banks and individuals to export silver if they wished, and asking them only to import an equal value of gold. Within six months, while the market price of silver was up, the job was mostly done, and with hardly a tremor El Salvador had converted to the gold standard.

In 1918 Venezuela reduced the silver content of her coins. In November 1919 the Netherlands reduced the fineness from .945 to .720. In January 1920 Canada reduced the fineness from .925 to .800.

The London price for silver hit $1.445 in October 1919 and stayed above that level (Britain's bullion parity) for four months. His Majesty's Government declared an embargo on silver exports and in March 1920 passed a law reducing the fineness from .925 to .500. That raised the bullion parity to $2.674. The new coins were issued in December 1920. They were yellowish and unpopular.

In France the silver coins disappeared when the market

price of silver went through France's bullion parity in 1919. The government passed laws forbidding the melting or exportation of coins. French shopkeepers and local Chambers of Commerce issued token money of brass, cardboard, and paper. The depreciated paper currency kept silver out of circulation after the market price of silver fell in 1920. Bronze-aluminum coins were minted in 2-franc, 1-franc, and half-franc denominations. Some observers estimated that the French citizenry were hoarding more than 2 billion francs in coins of gold and silver. Finally in September 1926 the government drew out the hoards by bidding 5.70 francs paper for 1 franc gold, and 2.40 francs paper for 1 franc silver. After two or three weeks the government's bid price for gold coins was lowered. Following the fall of the market price of silver the government ceased to offer a premium for silver coins. The franc was stabilized in 1928 at a new silver bullion parity of $1.790.

Thirty-three countries reduced the silver content of their coins between 1919 and 1933, and six countries abandoned silver coinage entirely.[1]

The Treasury of the U.S. faced a problem that was complex and highly ramified. The consequences of a faulty move might be serious and might be felt throughout the Free World. It was the kind of problem that had been met, with varying degrees of success, by every major country that had silver coinage at the beginning of the century. But the steps those countries had taken hardly seemed appropriate to the largest and most powerful country in the world. (Three-cent banknotes had disgraced the nation a century ago.) Such steps, in 1965, could undermine the international credit of the U.S.

And there was another element: the vending machines. Very effective public relations work had been done by the vending machine industry. Everyone was convinced that whatever decision the Treasury made would have to take full account of the problems of the coin-operated machines. To some extent this was true. A new coinage that would be too easily duplicated in weight and electrical conductivity would be a death-warrant for the vending machine operators. A new coinage that required radical adjustment of the rejection mechanisms would cost the industry a good deal of money (as much as $100 million, some said). Such objections were valid, but valid mainly for the operators of vending machines. From the standpoint of the national policy, a few million dollars spent retooling the rejection mechanisms of the vending machines were as nothing when compared with the international monetary disaster that seemed to be latent in the situation. Indeed, the entire vending machine business might have been sacrificed without irreparable damage to the United States. The $4 billion of annual sales chalked up by vending machines would not actually be lost to the general economy—the items not sold through machines would be sold, but in some other way, perhaps even in that magical fashion now known as people-to-people. The manufacturers of vending machines would lose the domestic market, and that would hurt; but the world is their oyster, and time cures all. Assets would have to be re-allocated. It was at least theoretically conceivable that the domestic vending machine business could be tossed overboard along with the silver coinage. Not pretty the prospect, nor happy the analyst, but there it is anyhow. In all such cases the guiding rule should be to disturb as little as possible of what is already established. John Randolph of Roanoke made it his first principle of politics: Disturb not that which is at rest. Economic theory says nothing of the brute fixities of life as it is lived. Even though the vending machine business should not be allowed to stand in the way of a new coinage for the country, still there is much to be said for keeping a large part of the retail structure in mind when altering the coinage it thrives upon. The plea of the machine vendors was theoretically impure, but politically right and good.

Two other elements made themselves felt at the Treasury: the silver miners and the silver users. The miners, of course, wanted to get a favorable price for their silver. To them that meant keeping as many buyers in the market as possible. Therefore they argued that the Treasury should keep some silver in the coinage. They based their argument on tradition (the bullion parity of the silver dollar was established by Alexander Hamilton), economics (a sound coin must have intrinsic worth), and psychology (the American people will become unhappy if they are deprived of their sound silver coinage). The economic argument is empty; we would have a much sounder monetary system if the paper money were convertible into gold and the coinage were mere aluminum; it is not the metal of the *subsidiary* money that determines the soundness of the money system. The argument from psychology is a matter of opinion; the historical record suggests that people accustom themselves rather promptly to a new coinage of reduced bullion value. The argument from tradition is the most respectable one the silver miners had available. Yes, it was a damned shame to depart from the monetary standard set by Alexander Hamilton. But silver dollars had never been very popular; Hamilton himself favored gold; and silver has now become a commercial and military commodity of great importance. The facts in the case appear to be absolutely commanding: there is not enough silver to go around. And, when all is said and done, the miners never explained what they thought would happen if silver were abolished from the coinage. It is perfectly clear that the price of silver will go up; in any case the miners will be getting more and more per ounce. In actual fact the miners have little to lose, and in the long run they can count on the most orderly and continuous rise in the price of silver if it is *not* tied to the bullion parity of some reduced-content U.S. coinage.

On the other side from the miners were, of course, the users. They argued that the supply and demand of silver require that it be dropped from the coinage entirely, so that the entire production might be devoted to the new and important industrial and military uses. If this were done, the Treasury's great hoard of silver (and, if melting occurred, then also the great hoard of silver tied up in the coinage) would become available for industrial use, and the silverware makers would be assured of a good supply and the best possible price. Their end of the silver business was highly sensitive to changes of price. They pointed out that in the decade ending in 1963 the price of silver went up 52 per cent and the unit sales of sterling flatware went down 48 per cent.[2] They pointed out that the market cost of silver accounts for 75 per cent of the end-price of sterling ware. The users wisely argued from the standpoint of the long-term interest of the nation. If silver were not eliminated entirely from the coinage, but were continued at some reduced level, then sooner or later, they argued, the whole problem would come up again. A stop-gap measure that would defer the problem for 30 years compared very unfavorably with the plans of Alexander Hamilton, which had lasted almost two centuries. To avoid a swift repetition of the monetary discomforts of the 1960s, they said, silver should be eliminated from the coinage once and for all.

To eliminate silver from the coinage would be a tremendous shock, as everyone admitted who was close to the problem. Silver had not only been in our coins since 1792, but in recent years an enormous acceleration in silver coinage had been the prime goal of Treasury policy. Mint production of domestic coin, excluding proof sets, had been as follows in recent years:

(Millions of pieces)[3]

Calendar Year	Halves	Quarters	Dimes	Nickels	Pennies
1954	44	109	243	194	419
1955	2	21	45	82	938
1956	4	76	217	102	1,519
1957	25	124	274	175	1,334
1958	28	84	168	185	1,053
1959	19	86	251	188	1,889
1960	24	92	271	248	2,167
1961	29	121	303	303	2,507
1962	45	164	407	378	2,399
1963	89	210	545	453	2,528
1964	202	382	811	797	3,384

Merely from the standpoint of bureacratic inertia, it was difficult to see how a policy of infinitely increasing silver coinage could be altered overnight to a policy of zero silver coinage. Secretary Dillon had been so closely associated with the "crash" coin production program that it was probably politically necessary for him to resign before the Treasury could honestly set forth the opposite policy.

Another problem has to do with the sheer size and complexity of the minting process. Silver bullion is acquired through purchases (ever less frequent) on the open market, through the retirement of old and worn coins, or from Treasury reserves. In an alloy with 10 per cent copper it is cast in hefty bars. These bars are run through rollers, as many as 22 sets of rollers, to produce strip of just the right thickness. Multiple punches then punch out plain round blanks from the silver strip. The blanks are heated in a gas flame ("annealed"). Then they are polished, washed, dried (centrifugally). They pass through another rolling process which thickens the edge of the blanks. After that stage they are weighed (and those that are not within rather narrow limits are rejected). The final production step is to take the blanks that have passed muster, and run them through the stamping machine, which puts the reeded (milled) pattern on the thickened edge and stamps the obverse and reverse designs on the two faces of the new coin. Machinery that can perform this operation on several billion coins a year had to be changed.[4]

At present there are U.S. mints at Denver and Philadelphia. Since the early 1920s the Treasury has had nothing to do with the distribution of coins except the proof sets sold directly to collectors. Newly minted coins are counted, bagged, and shipped to the Federal Reserve System, which exercises the power to distribute the coins among its twelve Federal Reserve Banks and 24 branches. The Federal Reserve Banks and branches deliver coin on request (and if available) to the commercial banks that are members of the Federal Reserve System. Those banks, in turn, ship coin (if available) to the banks that are not members of the Federal Reserve System (there are about 8,000 non-member banks).

The House Committee on Government Operations provided a good picture of the general problems attendant upon an alteration in the coinage:

The principal public consideration, of course, is that any change-over to new coinage be effected without disrupting the economy.

To that end, numerous considerations must be taken into account, such as to assure, as far as possible, that presently existing coin does not go out of circulation and that the new coinage be produced in sufficient quantities and be of such nature that public coin needs will be met. For instance, means must be considered to stop existing subsidiary coins from being melted down or withdrawn from circulation because of their silver content. Advocates of the retention of some silver in coin content claim this would make it less likely that presently existing silver coin would disappear from circulation. Advocates of removing all silver content claim that this would relieve the pressures entirely on the silver supply, and that speculators would probably dump their holdings, with the effect of forcing down the price of silver. Further, that if consideration be given to reducing the silver content at all, it would be well to entirely remove it; that otherwise the basic problem would continue, with further reductions being sought from time to time. In addition, they claim, there would be further pressures on the coin supply created by the demands of collectors for new sets of coins.

The effect, if any, of the economic doctrine known as Gresham's Law, that bad money tends to drive good money out of circulation, must be weighed. Whether or not it has any application to the U.S. coin system, the Treasury study must consider, when there is pressure on the price of silver so that it tends upward, speculators will gamble that the price will reach a point at which it becomes profitable to melt silver coin. Also, so long as there are purchasers willing to pay more for a coin than its face or intrinsic value, the tendency will be for that coin to stay out of circulation. If coin having silver content were to be withdrawn from circulation there would be a loss of approximately 1.925 billion ounces of silver.

The Treasury must also assure that its recommendations will be such as to provide adequate safeguards against counterfeiting and that it will provide coins compatible with present vending, toll, and other coin using devices.

The psychological problem of the reaction of the public to reducing or eliminating high intrinsic value of coin content must also be assessed. Many contend that coins must have an intrinsic value in order to maintain confidence in the coin, and also confidence in our paper money. Others claim there is no need for any intrinsic value in coins because their main function is to serve as useful means of exchange.

Coin is not intended to be a commodity. The present coin shortage, however, is due in part to the fact that the intrinsic value of silver coin is so high that it lends itself to speculation. As such, coin becomes more valuable as a commodity than as a medium of exchange.[5]

The fascinating thing about that summary is that it appears to have been written in disregard of the historical record. As our review of the experience of other countries has shown, there would seem to be very little that a government can do once its coinage is at the melting point. The coinage will disappear, either because the government buys it in at a premium (France) or because it is exported or melted (Mexico, China, etc.). Yet the committee report seems to assume that It Can't Happen Here. If this kind of confidence is something beyond the necessary air of "masterly inactivity" that characterizes a statesman while he prepares a stunning stratagem in the midst of chaos, if we should take it at face value—then it's a fair guess that many gentlemen in high position will be astonished at the turn of events. One authoritative institute has estimated that one-third of the outstanding U.S. silver coinage is now in hoards.[6] That the U.S. economy could snap up the whole silver currency is apparent from the simplest calculations: the face value of the silver coinage amounts to one-third of one per cent of the Gross National Product, or about $12 per person. In comparison, the money supply (i.e., *all* forms of purchasing media) amounts to about $800 per person.

Thus the problems, as seen from close up. We now turn to a consideration of the steps that the Government has taken in recent months to meet the situation. This will involve an analysis of the Treasury report, of the President's message to Congress, and of the new coinage law.

6. President Johnson Flunks Out

ON JUNE 3, 1965, the Congress received a message from President Johnson concerning silver coinage and recommending new legislation. The message from the President got off to a bad start with its very first sentence:

From the early days of our independence the United States has used a system of coinage fully equal in quantity and quality to all the tasks imposed upon it by the Nation's commerce.[1]

If we exempt President Jefferson's troubles with the silver dollar as falling outside President Johnson's formula ("From the early days...."), we still must admit that we have gone through two major periods of coin shortage serious enough to impel Washington to issue fractional scrip, and the string of lesser banking panics rounds out a picture of something far different from the monetary paradise described by the President. He continues:

We are today using one of the few existing silver coinages in the world.

Irrelevant. We are also using one of the few existing systems of truly universal public schooling—but that is no reason for abandoning it. The statement is also misleading. Canada, France, Italy, Japan, Germany, and other countries continued to use silver in their coinage in 1964 and 1965; and the total use of silver in Free World coinage outside the U.S. was up more than 20 per cent in 1964 above the 1962 level (it was down 25 per cent from 1961, but up 7 per cent from 1960).[2] It would have been better if the President had said: "Underdeveloped countries, and countries subject to centralized economic control, do not use silver coinage. Many of the industrially advanced countries, including the U.S., do."

...The long tradition of our silver coinage is one of the many marks of the extraordinary stability of our political and economic system.

Our monetary system has enjoyed considerable stability, but it can be viewed from quite another perspective. The President might just as well have said: "For the first 141 years we were on the gold standard, with silver dancing the awkward partner in a bimetallic minuet. Then in 1933 we abandoned gold in order to engage in monetary inflation. The price level has quadrupled. Now silver must go too."

Continuity, however, is not the only characteristic of a great nation's coinage.

Correct. There are other characteristics, such as 1) convertibility into precious metals, 2) convertibility into foreign currencies, 3) stability of purchasing power over the years. The dollar has lost No. 3, is losing No. 2 through "voluntary" programs, and is losing No. 1 as silver joins gold among the unattainables. Now it will lose "continuity." What remains of the great nation's coinage?

We should not hesitate to change our coinage to meet new and growing needs.

If they are *needs,* then one agrees of course. To the extent that the situation arises from inflation, one is permitted to ask whether inflation is a necessity. If, in any case, the claims can be admitted to be *needs,* then they are needs whether they be "new" or "growing" or not. A need is none the less needful for being new, and none the less needful for being on the ascendant. It so happens that the President is half right in this sentence. External events have imposed a condition upon our system of coinage: the free market demand for silver is strong enough to deplete the Treasury supplies of silver as long as we keep monetizing silver at $1.29 and/ or $1.38 an ounce. There is, then, an iron-clad condition laid upon the monetary authorities. In the absence of dictatorial control over the entire world silver market, they must abandon their present notion of the "value" of silver, and either fix a new and higher bullion parity to the coinage, or abandon silver entirely.

... There has been for some years a worldwide shortage of silver.

Yes.

The United States is not exempt from that shortage—and we will not be exempt as it worsens.

If this is a pledge from the President that there shall be no attempts at artificial exemption through tariffs, end-use certificates, special taxation on silver transactions, and similar laws with which the New Deal experimented in the 1930s and later—then this country may be said to have learned from experience and taken a step forward.

Silver is becoming too scarce for continued large-scale use in coins.

I believe that to be true, but my assent is an act of faith because the statement is inexact. Every commodity is of course *scarce*. Human beings measure scarcity against a scale of their own choosing, such as the cost of acquisition. The cost of acquiring an ounce of silver has now risen to the point where one has one's choice: either dig the ore, or convert paper money into a silver dollar. People, being motivated by a sense of efficiency (which misanthropes call sloth), will convert paper to coin sooner than dig in the earth. Thus the coin tends to disappear from circulation. The price of silver in the free market is such that the metal can no longer stay in circulation if we call an ounce of it worth $1.29 in face value of money. However, *silver has always been scarce, and that is why it has always been a monetary metal.* The brute fact of scarcity is not an argument against, but an argument in favor of, the monetization of a commodity. The question is always: What rate should the commodity be monetized at? That is the question of silver now. Should it be demonetized entirely, or should the dollar be devalued in relation to silver?

To maintain unchanged our high silver coinage in the face of this stark reality would only invite a chronic and growing scarcity of coins.

Actually, it would be impossible to *maintain* the present coinage. We might prolong it, but only so long as the Treasury's reserves of silver might hold out. After that point we do not coin at the old rate any more. The official ("monetary") price of silver moves up to the next plateau.

...We must take steps to maintain an adequate supply of coins, or face chaos in the myriad transactions of our daily life—from using pay telephones to parking in a metered zone to providing our children with money for lunch at school.

The examples the President has chosen are brilliantly apt. They illustrate the inconceivable variety of events and trans- actions that depend for the moment upon a certain coinage. But I would displace his emphasis quite a bit. If we had no coinage at all, I am sure that we could invent a way of get- ting on with things. Approximately 98 per cent of our busi- ness life is conducted on faith at the moment, and it might be a good thing if we learned how to conduct all of it on faith. A check at the end of the month, payable to the man on the street corner who sells you your morning newspaper— what is unthinkable about that? And who is to say that we might not all be the gainers? For it is easy to assume that a society is prosperous and happy in proportion to the amount of its business that it can conduct on the basis of trust. Gov- ernment, by guaranteeing the value of the coinage, has served as the intermediary in transactions, saying: Don't you and he trust each other; both of you must trust me; I shall stand bail for this contract;...and so a dollar, or a pound note, changes hands. It would be more direct if the parties to a contract were required to be men of good faith, and to know each other. There would be less opening for the smart player to ride on to fortune on the generally accepted credit of the government that issues the notes.

The legislation I am sending to the Congress with this message will insure a stable and dignified coinage...

There is no record in human history of a coinage that has been absolutely stable. Some have been more stable than others, but every coinage has fallen after this length of time or that. So it may be an exaggeration on the part of the President when he promises that his legislative proposal will "insure" a stable coinage. Mayhap it will endure for ten or 20 years. That will not earn it any award for durability, when we think of the byzant, for example, which maintained its silver content unchanged for almost a thousand years.[3] As to a "dignified" coinage, I have no idea what the President means. Human dignity is a function of the intrinsic value of the individual; the President seems to be saying that dignity in coinage may be arrived at by depriving the coinage of all intrinsic value and making it dependent upon outside agencies for its acceptability. *Dignitas*: worth, worthiness, merit.

...fully adequate in quantity and in its specially designed technical characteristics to the needs of our twentieth century life. It can be maintained indefinitely, however much the demand for coin may grow.

Surely an exaggeration. How do we know that the new coinage can be maintained "indefinitely"? Within 30 years, if the U.S. inflation continues at the present pace, what now costs a quarter will cost a half-dollar. Thirty years from now, therefore, the 40 per cent silver half-dollar (recommended in this message by the President) will become our principal coin. Shall we have some great new source of silver then? The President himself says, further on in his message, that we cannot look forward to discovering great new sources of silver. Therefore his words must be construed as either 1) a promise to put a final end to the 40-year inflation, or 2) an exaggeration of the longevity of the new coinage. The second is more likely.

I propose no change in either the penny or the nickel.

Changes have been known to occur even without their having been proposed by the President. The price of silver has almost quintupled since 1932, thanks to the twin forces of industrial growth and monetary inflation. If the price of copper should quintuple in the next 30 years, then the copper in a penny would be worth exactly one cent—and our penny population would disappear, just as our silver dollars have.

The new dime and the quarter—while remaining the same size and design as the present dime and quarter—will be composite coins. They will have faces of the same copper-nickel alloy used in our present 5-cent piece, bonded to a core of pure copper. The new dime and quarter will, therefore, outwardly resemble the nickel, except in size and design, but with the further distinction that their copper core will give them a copper edge.

Viewed from the edge, the new "clad" coin look like a salami sandwich made with mouldy bread.

This type of coin was selected because, alone among practical alternatives, it can be used together with our existing silver coins in the millions of coin-operated devices that Americans now depend upon....

Same density, same electrical conductivity.

Our new half-dollar will be nearly indistinguishable in appearance from the present half-dollar.

If the new half-dollar appears at all, it will be distinguished: the present half-dollar is disappearing.

It will continue to be made of silver and copper, but the silver content will be reduced from 90 to 40 per cent. It will be faced with an alloy of 80 per cent silver and 20 per cent copper, bonded to a core of 21 per cent silver and 79 per cent copper. The new half-dollar will continue to be minted with the image of President Kennedy. Its size will be unchanged.

The high silver content of the external covering is in memory of the superficial glitter of the Kennedy years. The debased core will remind us that President Kennedy was one of our greatest inflationists. As I pointed out above, it is entirely possible that even this debased coin will be driven from circulation in 30 years or so, assuming a continuation of the present inflation. The coin might disappear even sooner if the Treasury takes the lid off the silver market. Some analysts think the free market price of silver would be $4 an ounce in the absence of Treasury dumping. When silver hits $3.11 an ounce, the new debased half-dollar will head for the melting pots.

[The silver dollar]: No change in this famous old coin, or plans for additional production, are proposed at this time.

Ten days earlier, the President announced that he had ordered the Mint to proceed with the production of 45 million silver dollars.[4] A Treasury official followed up with the statement that the new silver dollars would bear the familiar design of the Peace dollar minted from 1921 to 1935, would be minted at the Denver Mint, and would bear the date 1964. The Treasury official added that the explanation for the decision would be found in the forthcoming Treasury report on silver and the coinage.[5] This was, as things turned out, a lie. The Treasury report made it clear that silver should be abandoned entirely. The mid-May maneuver by the Treasury and the White House must be considered as a propaganda maneuver to forestall speculation against the currency—akin to the repeated declarations that a currency is perfectly sound, which take place immediately before devaluation.

It is possible that implementation of the new coinage legislation that I am proposing, greatly reducing the requirement for silver in our subsidiary coinage, will actually make feasible the minting of additional silver dollars in the future.

This seems to be a direct contradiction of the President's statement, elsewhere in the message, that "Much as we all would prefer to retain the silver coins now in use, there is no practical alternative to a new coinage based on materials in adequate supply."

Certainly, without this change in the silver content of the subsidiary coinage, further minting of the silver dollar would be forever foreclosed.

Arguing in a circle. Having pointed out that X is impossible under ideal conditions, the President asserts that X is also impossible under conditions less than ideal. But he does so in a way that suggests that if conditions could only be improved, X might become possible. Which is impossible.

It is our intention that the new coinage circulate side by side with our existing coinage.

You have in your hand two quarters. One contains 25 cents' worth of silver, the other has only a few cents' worth of copper and nickel. You owe me a quarter. Which one do you give me? When there is a really significant difference between the intrinsic values of two coins that have the same debt-paying value, the more valuable one tends to be hung onto, and the less valuable one tends to be used in circulation. This is, more or less, a statement of Gresham's Law (which the reader may pursue further in any encyclopaedia or economics text). The American people have acted many times in the past in accordance with Gresham's Law. The odds are that the President's "intention" will be frustrated.

We plan to continue the minting of our current silver coins while the new coinage is brought into quantity production.

The Administration chooses the lesser of evils. It announces that there is not enough silver for continued coinage, but at the same time it announces that it will continue to coin silver. This it does because the alternative would be worse. The alternative would be to announce that all silver coining will now stop. The effect of such an announcement might be a serious coin shortage, for two reasons: 1) the new non-silver coinage would not be in production, and 2) the old silver coinage might tend to be held by speculators in the hope that it might acquire a scarcity value.

The new coins will be placed in circulation some time in 1966.

There are about 13 billion pieces of the old silver coinage outstanding. The Administration expects to work up an inventory of several billion pieces of the new coinage and then unload it at once into the banking system, so that the new coinage will not be withheld from circulation on account of its scarcity value. By mid-1967 the Administration hopes to have produced about 11 billion pieces of new non-silver coinage, mostly dimes and quarters—enough, therefore, to replace almost entirely the old silver coinage. The country will be flooded with enormous quantities of the new and intrinsically almost valueless coinage. What will happen to the old, silver, "good" coinage? In any case the forecast was wrong; after 200 million cupronickel quarters had been minted, they went into circulation not in 1966 but in November 1965. By year-end, 400 million of the new quarters had been minted.

...I want to make it absolutely clear that these changes in our coinage will have no effect on the purchasing power of our coins.

True, but irrelevant. If the new coinage becomes as common as the grains of sand on the beach, its purchasing power will be as that of the grains of sand. If the price of silver goes up very much, the old coinage will have a purchasing power much higher than that of the new coinage. Clearly the quantity of production of the new coinage, and the future course of the market price of silver, are not controlled by the legislation here being recommended. Hence the President can sound very firm and reassuring while actually uttering a completely irrelevant statement. There is, actually, no reason at all to feel reassured concerning the future purchasing power of a currency whose value rests entirely upon the good faith of an Administration which is characterized by false dealing.

...The legislation I am proposing expressly recognizes the new coins as legal tender.

This is said in support of the reassurance about "purchasing power of our coins." But there is no connection between the purchasing power of a currency and its status as legal tender. The German mark was legal tender in 1922 and 1923 even while it was inflated on an incredible scale (1 to 230 billion in a year). It became worthless; it remained legal tender. The President's argument that whatever is legal tender is therefore of constant purchasing power is either ignorant or disingenuous.

It is of primary importance, of course, that our new coins be specifically designed to serve our modern, technological society.

"Of course"? The meaning here is that it is of primary importance that our coins have a certain electrical conductivity. This is *not* of primary importance. But it would have seemed obviously ridiculous to speak of electrical conductivity as the primary feature of a good coinage. Hence the god-words "our modern, technological society." The President goes on:

In the early days of the Republic, silver coins served well because the value of a coin could only be measured by the value of the precious metal contained in it.

Silver coins did *not* serve well in the early days, as we have already pointed out. President Johnson slides from one sense of the word "value" to a different sense without warning. "Face value" can always be unrelated to intrinsic value: that is what allows paper money to circulate. "Purchasing value" or purchasing power is *always* related to a physical commodity and is measured by it. A mark is a mark is a mark; it says so right there in print; even when it takes 230 billion marks to buy something that cost only one mark the year before.

For many decades now the value of a particular coin has depended not on the value of the metal in it, but on the face value of the coin.

This is meaningless. If President Johnson intends to say that the face value depends upon the face value, then his statement is a mere tautology. If he means to say that purchasing power depends upon face value, he is wrong. If he means that intrinsic value depends upon face value, he is wrong again. He continues:

Today's coinage must primarily be utilitarian.

Why only *today's* coinage? It seems odd that only now should we require a coinage to be useful—as if all of the past had been an age in which men gladly accepted a useless coinage. Does President Johnson mean "useful" when he says "utilitarian"? Solid silver is useful, and is becoming increasingly useful in our "modern, technological society." Silver has become "utilitarian." *Therefore* it must not be used in a coinage which, nevertheless, "must primarily be utilitarian." Such is the chaos of President Johnson's message. He continues:

The new coinage will meet this requirement fully...

Here again a seemingly strong assertion trails off into vacuity upon examination. What "requirement" is being met, and in what way is it being met "fully"?

...while dispensing with the idea that it contain precious metal.

No coinage, old or new, can dispense with ideas. It is people who dispense with ideas, accepting them or rejecting them. President Johnson undoubtedly rejects the idea that a coinage should possess intrinsic value.

It is, above all, practical. It has been specifically designed to function, without causing delays or disruptions of service, in coin-operated merchandising machines.

So *that* is what "utilitarian" means! The *primary* requirement of "today's coinage" is that it create no inconvenience to the operators of vending machines!

The President goes on in his message to review the findings of the Treasury study. The principal finding, which has to do with the new industrial uses of silver, is an echo of the article written ten years earlier by John Chamberlain.

...Our silver coins are protected by the fact that the Government stands ready to sell silver bullion from its stocks at $1.29 a troy ounce. This keeps the price of silver, as a commodity, from rising above the face value of our coins.

Not at all. It keeps the market value of the coins, as a commodity, from rising above their face value. The President's language is entirely wrong. However, it would not do to accuse him of ignorance on this point. Quite possibly this erroneous and misleading phrase was chosen deliberately in order to avoid stating the clear possibility that the old silver coinage might be worth more as silver than as coin some day.

This, in turn, makes hoarding or melting of the silver coinage unprofitable.

Not precisely. It makes the *liquidation* of speculative hoards unprofitable. It does nothing to avert the *accumulation* of speculative hoards based on the presumption that the Treasury will not forever be able to hold the price of silver below its free-market economic level.

...We believe our present stocks of silver to be adequate, once the large present drains from coinage are greatly reduced, to meet any foreseeable requirements for an indefinite period.

For an indefinite period! The President is joking, surely. Mr. Francis H. Wemple, treasurer of Handy & Harman, has testified (June, 1965: House Banking and Currency Committee) to the opposite: "Let's examine the Treasury stock situation by 1970. According to the President's message the new coins will not go into circulation until sometime in 1966. Therefore we may assume that mid-1966 may be the time. Treasury stocks now amount to about 1,000,000,000 ounces. At the present rate of use they will be down to about 580,-000,000 ounces by the middle of next year. After deducting the proposed stockpile of 135,000,000 ounces, there would be less than 450,000,000 ounces left, which at the present rate of redemptions as well as projected use for half-dollars would be gone before 1970." If President Johnson believes that a period of less than five years is an "indefinite period," then he is short-sighted indeed. The President continues:

However, prompt action on a new coinage will help us protect the silver coinage by freeing our silver reserves for redemption of silver certificates at $1.29 per ounce. Thus, we can assure that no incentive will be created for hoarding our present coins in anticipation of a higher price for their silver content. [Emphasis his.]

"However" or "therefore"? And once again, if we accept the extrapolations by Mr. Wemple, we shall find little reason to share the optimism of President Johnson.

...We are convinced that we can include a 40 per cent silver half-dollar in the new coinage, but we cannot safely go beyond that. As a precaution, we intend to concentrate at first on getting out large quantities of the new quarter and dime before we embark upon quantity production of the new half-dollar.

On the surface this is perfectly reasonable. The Treasury estimated that by year-end 1965 there would be outstanding about 7.8 billion dimes, 3.3 billion quarters, and 1.2 billion halves, all of the old "good" silver mintage.[6] The immediate goal of the crash production effort would be to replace the bulk of the silver coinage, and the bulk of it is in dimes and quarters. Reasonable or not, the promise was broken before the year was out. Even before the new dimes were in circulation, and when only one new quarter had been minted for every eight in circulation, the Mint commenced production of the new debased Kennedy halves.

As Mr. Wemple points out, it is unlikely that the Treasury will be able to produce the new 40 per cent silver half-dollar for very long. It would run out of silver in 1970 or so. That would mean that only a small number of the 40-per-cent-silver Kennedy halves would be issued. They would therefore acquire quite a scarcity value. They would go into the safekeeping troves of the nation, just as the Kennedy halves have done so far, and whatever silver was used in them would be silver lost from the Treasury and not effectively in circulation anyway. From the standpoint of the Treasury that would be a dead loss. However, individual citizens should, it seems, keep their eyes peeled for the new Kennedy halves. They may very well be scarcer than the original issue.

The President's legislative proposal also provided for the creation of a Joint Commission on the Coinage. Its chairman would be the Secretary of the Treasury. Other members would be the Secretary of Commerce; the Director of the Bureau of the Budget; the Director of the Mint; the chairman and the ranking minority member of the Senate Banking and Currency Committee; the same functionaries of the House Banking and Currency Committee; one member of the House appointed by the Speaker; one member of the Senate appointed by the President of the Senate; and four public members appointed by the President. The duties of the Joint Commission on the Coinage would be to review "from time to time such matters as the needs of the economy for coins, the standards for the coinage, technological developments in metallurgy and coin-selector devices, the availability of various metals, renewed minting of the silver dollar, the time when and circumstances under which the United States should cease to maintain the price of silver, and other considerations relevant to the maintenance of an adequate and stable coinage system."

The Congress should have looked very closely at this proposal. It creates a commission of 14 members, eight of whom are picked by the President. The commission, as a result of the number and eminence of its members, may be expected to speak with great authority on monetary matters. And, as a result of the President's having appointed eight of the 14 commission members, we may expect that the opinion of the President will acquire, through this means, a great new charge of authoritativeness in these areas. The Congress should have studied this proposal the more carefully because these areas, in which the White House appears to be greatly amplifying its power, include one area that is very specifically placed under the control not of the President but of the Congress. The Constitution (Article I, Section 8) gives to the Congress the "power...to coin money, regulate the value thereof...."

Here, instead, is a commission, in effect a Presidential commission, created to serve without time limit, charged with all the authority of high officials of cabinet and Congress, which will guide the coinage and even have a say in the decision that will abolish the old silver coinage. In theory, of course, it may always be contended that Congress preserves the power to override the Joint Commission. But when the Speaker of the House and the President of the Senate each have a man on the Commission, the chances of Congressional independence look still slimmer.

There is one further point in the legislative proposal that merits special attention. Title I, Section 5 provides: "Whenever in the judgment of the Secretary of the Treasury such action is necessary to protect the coinage of the United States, he is authorized under such rules and regulations as he may prescribe to prohibit the exportation, melting or treating of coins of the United States." Violators may be fined (Section 16) $10,000 and jailed for five years. This is the kind of law that works against the long-term interest of the law-givers. The long-term interest of the law-givers is to put into circulation a coinage not subject to the currently disruptive forces of the silver market, and to make as much silver as possible available to the free market for purposes industrial, military, artistic, or whatever. *Over the long term* the Government has no interest in keeping silver *per se* in the hands of the public. Yet, if Gresham's Law begins to operate in the next few years, millions of private citizens will salt away a sockful of the old, "good" silver dimes or quarters or even halves (if they can find them), and the old silver coinage will disappear. Congressman Craig Hosmer predicted just that, without qualifications, in a June 10 letter to his fellow Congressmen. If this happens as Mr. Hosmer says it will, then one of the largest aggregations of silver in the world will not only be locked up and kept on ice—but according to the law there will be severe penalties for making it available on the free market, even while the market (if not the Government also) is starving for silver, and bidding the price up hand over fist. Some 2.2 billion ounces of silver are tied up in the silver coinage now in the hands of the American people. When there are enough pieces of the new non-silver coinage to supplant the old coinage in all normal channels of commerce, then provision should be made for the entry of the old silver coinage back into the silver market. If the Treasury is interested in keeping the price of silver from going through the roof, the best thing it could do would be to provide for the melting and sale of 2.2 billion ounces of silver now held by American citizens. If the preservation of silver coin and the melting of it for profit is made illegal in this country, then the experience of many nations would lead us to assume that a great share of the silver hoard will make its way illegally to foreign countries, there to be melted. U.S. purchases of foreign silver would add pressure on our current payments deficit. Once again, the long-term interest of the U.S. would be thwarted.

The President sent his coinage proposals to Congress on June 3, 1965. The Senate Banking and Currency Committee approved them on June 9, the Senate as a whole on June 24. The House passed the bill on July 14 with minor changes. On July 15 the Senate accepted those changes and forwarded the bill to the President. On July 23 President Johnson signed the bill, assuring the masses that there "very definitely" would not be any disappearance of the old silver coinage "for many, many years to come."[7]

7.   An Opportunity Missed

HAVING GIVEN some attention to the President's coinage message and to various provisions of the proposed coinage legislation, I should like to deal now with the principal element in the Coinage Act of 1965—the abandonment of silver from our coinage. I am not competent to judge whether the new material is the best that could be found, but I shall assume that it is, because the selection of a coinage that would satisfy the requirements of a "modern, technological" society would proceed along lines uninfluenced by a philosophy of money. Which is to say, if a laboratory experimentalist at Battelle Memorial Institute is to decide *only* among various elements that have been selected previously on the grounds that they are of little intrinsic value, then the decision made in the laboratory—a second-stage decision—says nothing about the question of intrinsic value. Von Mises, in his *Theory of Money and Credit,* ignores the question of coinage materials on the ground that it is of merely "technical," not "economic" importance.

I would enter only one note of apprehension concerning the new coins. (I assume the partly silver Kennedy half will not be minted in quantity.) This has to do with the cost of manufacturing them. Official statements are somewhat vague about the cost of manufacture. ("Cost estimates are not yet entirely firm..."[1]). It is possible that the new coins will turn out to be more expensive to make than our experts had calculated. Whenever it costs more than the face value of a coin to manufacture that coin, the manufacturing comes to a halt. If the experience of minting the new coins shows that we are well on our way towards that point, then it seems clear that the new coinage will not last a great length of time but will have to be abandoned in turn, to be supplanted by some ultra-new coinage (which will no doubt be ultra-modern and ultra-technological).

Be this as it may, the prior question of intrinsic value remains to be discussed. I may as well begin with a statement of position on the subject by a well-known columnist, Miss Sylvia Porter:

Q. Without silver, what will back our coins?
A. The same power, ability, capacity, and faith which back all our money—both paper and coins. This is the power of our economy. This is the ability of the U.S. as a nation, and of us as individual U.S. citizens, to produce, to earn, to trade, to grow. This is the faith we have in our power, ability and capacity.[2]

Here Miss Porter gives voice, and not without a certain naive eloquence, to an economic proposition that actually has enjoyed a great vogue for many years. I do not know whether the proposition in this exact form has ever been seriously analyzed, but I should imagine that any analysis of it must begin with the question: Precisely how does the industrial power of the United States contribute to the stability of our monetary unit?

Now that question can be translated into concrete terms. Miss Porter says that if we all produce, earn, trade, and "grow," then our monetary unit will be "backed." I accept the joyous picture of a nation plugging merrily away at its chores like a mass of Snow White's dwarfy friends, and I add one further element: a federal policy of unlimited printing of paper money. (I may add this element to Miss Porter's picture, because she has not required its exclusion.) We now have a nation happily operating its industrial machinery, but paved from coast to coast with dollar bills, let's say up to *here*. Our industrial plant remains as it was when Miss Porter declared that it was backing the currency, but our currency is now free for the asking; bend over and scoop up a handful of dollar bills on your way to work. What happens to the purchasing power of the dollar?

Well, of course I have not done full justice to Miss Porter's exposition. She goes on immediately after the passage I have already quoted, concluding her article (the third of a three-part series on the new coinage) as follows:

Fundamentally, the worth of your paper currency and metal coins will be determined by the amounts of goods and services your money can buy for you. Against this yardstick, a vault of silver bars behind the paper or a pinch of silver in the coin just aren't comparable.

The underlying meaning of that statement is in violent contrast to Miss Porter's preceding sentences. Here she admits that the existence of a smoothly humming industrial civilization is not enough, in itself, to guarantee ("back," "determine") the purchasing power of the currency. The purchasing power is "determined" by the amounts of goods and services that can be purchased per unit of currency—says Miss Porter—and here she stumbles into a circular argument. The purchasing power may certainly be *measured* by the money price of economic goods, but that is because the money price is an aspect, not a cause, not a determinant, of the purchasing power of currency.

So the argument, in Miss Porter's hands, has come full circle. Asked about the backing of the currency, she replies that the industrial plant is our guarantee of stability. Recognizing that stability is measured by the money price level, she cancels her previous statement and says that the price level, "fundamentally," is guaranteed by—the price level.

But now, if we are to go along with Miss Porter, we must shift our ground a great deal from the first position. The "backing" of our currency is no longer our "faith...in our power, ability and capacity." That is, on Miss Porter's own showing, not enough. We must have faith in the public servants who are responsible for "regulating the value" of our money. Indeed, the only thing that "backs" a currency that has no tie to precious metals is the faith of the people in the currency itself; which is, at bottom, a faith that the managers of the currency will not debase it by excessive issue.

But I have allowed Miss Porter to draw us along too fast. The question of "backing" came up, at first, in the context of our abandoning silver coinage. The question is irrelevant in this narrow framework. The circulating small coin, the small change in a monetary system, is valuable primarily because of its *convenience* in making small transactions. If all available alternatives are sufficiently awkward, it is even theoretically possible that a small denomination coin will remain in circulation although its intrinsic value exceeds its face value. Indeed we have a recent example of this. The World War II nickel, with an intrinsic value of up to 7¢ in recent years, was very slow to disappear. If you knew that the nickel in your pocket was worth 7¢ at the smelter, which is 200 miles away, would you ship that nickel to the smelter, or buy a newspaper with it?

"Money" is not at all a perfectly defined term. It includes several different functions, and there is some reason to believe that the "thing" behind one function genuinely differs from the thing behind another. The various functions of "money" are commonly said to include, for example, 1) a medium of exchange, 2) a measurement of value, 3) a store of value, 4) a method of deferred payment. But the word of an honest man can serve as a medium of exchange, and pennies and farthings are seldom used as a *long-term* store of value (too bulky; counting problem; disbursing problem). Although one type of "money" shades off into another type without clear-cut distinctions, it is possible to make statements about the separate functions; and the further one function is removed from another, the more likely it is that differentiating statements may be made.

We have, then, on the one hand a question of small change, and on the other hand a question of the long-term store of value. Silver is being taken out of our small change. Does this event threaten the function of our "money" as a long-term store of value? Miss Porter fails to distinguish between the two separate aspects of "money," and that is why her statement, and my treatment of it, led us too swiftly along the pathway of discussion.

Intrinsic value has little to do with the suitability of coin in making small transactions. Small change might just as well be made of cardboard, as long as it is made in such a way as to be easily identifiable as genuine (difficult to counterfeit).

Small change should be made of a material available in great quantity (it would be folly to expose *precious* metals to the wear and tear of a dozen transactions a day). Small change should be made of a material cheap enough to allow the manufacture of a coin you can get your fingers on. A penny made of gold would be well-nigh invisible. Thus there is nothing fundamentally askew in the provisions of the Coinage Act of 1965 relating to the issue of new dimes and quarters (and, I am convinced, eventually new halves) without precious metal content.

Further, from the standpoint of cleaning up our currency, I am sure that most monetary theorists will welcome the departure of silver coinage and indeed of silver itself from the money system. Complexity is not in itself a desirable thing in a money system, and ours has a degree of complexity that is entirely out of line with the functions it performs. A Circulation Statement of the Treasury will show the following "Kinds of Money":

CURRENT:
>   gold
>   gold certificates—series of 1934
>   *standard silver dollars*
>   *silver bullion*
>   *silver certificates—issued after 6/30/29*
>   *subsidiary coin**
>   minor coin**
>   United States notes
>   Federal Reserve notes—1928 and subsequent series

---

*This category was reported as "subsidiary silver" until August 1965. After August the caption was changed to "subsidiary coin," covering halves, quarters, and dimes of the old silver content and of the new non-silver content indiscriminately.

**Nickels and pennies.

IN PROCESS OF RETIREMENT:
> Federal Reserve Bank notes
> National Bank notes
> gold certificates—prior to series of 1934
> Federal Reserve notes—prior to series of 1928
> *silver certificates—issued before 7/1/29*
> Treasury Notes of 1890

The departure of silver from this baffling list of kinds of money should be welcomed. I have, I hope, made clear the reasons why we should not regret the disappearance of silver from the coinage. I should also explain why the extinction of silver certificates and the Treasury's silver bullion monetary reserves should cause no panic.

The principal line of argument, in my opinion, has to do with the relative place of silver in the U.S. money supply. On June 30, 1965, the money supply was $161.7 billion. The silver component was $3.7 billion.[3] Silver, therefore, amounts to about 2.3 per cent of the money supply; or, to put it the other way around, our money supply is now about 97.7 per cent off silver. To take it entirely off silver will hardly affect the total money mechanism except to simplify it. From the standpoint of the monetary system as a whole, silver has never served as a guarantor of stability or as the conservator of the purchasing power of the currency. Instead, it has been the plaything of inflationists for the past century. If it is not required in the coinage and if it has never supported our money at the opposite end of the money spectrum (i.e., never supported it as a long-term store of value), then there is very little indeed to be said for silver, and a great deal to be said for the simplification that its departure might herald.

But we are not quit of the subject so handily. It may be

true that silver has never served as a guarantor for the money supply as a whole, but it is also true that in recent years it has been available to private citizens as an alternative to the paper currency. That this availability has not been unimportant to the citizens may be seen from the recent activity in silver dollars, subsidiary silver coins, and silver bullion itself. It may be true that a great deal of the activity is entirely speculative. But that does not rule out the possibility that some people, perhaps only a very few people, have genuinely preferred to convert part of their holdings into a liquid form that might preserve its purchasing power independently of the activities of the money managers. If a few people or many people desire to do this, it is difficult to find reasons why they should be deprived of the liberty to do so. That is why the contrary argument never takes the form of arguing that these people *must* be deprived of this liberty; it always takes the form (see Sylvia Porter, above) of arguing that the proposed activity is *unnecessary* (please notice that A takes it upon himself to decide what B needs), and therefore shall not be allowed. The argument is an evasion, but it continues to enjoy a great audience.

Intrinsic value has a great deal to do with the suitability of a currency as a long-term store of value. It is, as I have already mentioned, erroneous to argue from the requirements of small change to the attributes of a sound money system. No one would seriously maintain that a checking account should have a certain electrical conductivity just because the operators of vending machines use that test for rejecting coins. And yet there are those, such as Miss Porter and President Johnson, who argue from small change to the monetary system as a whole without changing their criteria. If intrinsic value is no longer important, necessary, desirable, or possible in the small change, they say—why, then, intrinsic value is no longer important in the monetary system as a whole!

Unfortunately for those who embrace that conclusion, the testimony of experience runs to the contrary. Only those moneys that have possessed close ties to intrinsic value have been able to serve as long-term stores of value. Except in climactic periods of chiliastic panic, people of all places and epochs have shown overriding interest in storing up value for the long term—perhaps to enjoy its purchasing power in their old age, or to bequeath its purchasing power to their descendants or friends. Certainly in any advanced society a system must be provided for the writing and settlement of long-term contracts, and the heart of any long-term contract is the assumption that the purchasing power represented by today's payment will be represented many years from now by the stipulated reimbursement. To measure the future purchasing power of today's tangible wealth, and to store up a portion of purchasing power, are fundamental and all-pervasive goals of human effort. And if the money system does not provide a method of future measurement and a store of value, then people will look for substitutes for those functions (even while using the money for today's small transactions).

In this light the Coinage Act of 1965 takes on a less healthy color. The removal of silver from our coinage system and from our monetary base took place only a few months after a major step was taken to divorce our money from gold. Early in 1965 the President signed a law that removed the great bulk of our purchasing media from even an indirect relation to the requirement of a 25 per cent gold backing. As a result, only the folding money (Federal Reserve Notes) is backed by gold, and the folding money is a small part of the total money supply—about $38 billion out of $162 billion.

There is absolutely no legal limit to the amount of checking-account money that can be created through the extension of various forms of bank credit. The only tie that our enormous total of money now has to anything of intrinsic value is the legal requirement that the Federal Reserve not issue folding money in excess of four times the amount of gold certificates on hand. That relation between gold and the folding money is tenuous itself, because the history of recent decades suggests that no administration would hesitate to reduce the reserve requirement in order to continue the monetary expansion. At the current rate of note issue and gold outflow, the gold reserve ratio will have to be reduced again within eighteen months. We now have, for the first time in American history, a money system that is *de facto* divorced from any serious relation to tangible value.

If it were necessary to have things this way, only a fool would balk. But I know of no persuasive arguments to this effect. Indeed the most persuasive argument in favor of making a money of intrinsic value available to the people is just this: that the people will sooner or later flee from the depreciating money, into goods of intrinsic value, anyway—and that it is easier for government to measure the timing and volume of the flight if it takes place in the gold vaults of the banking system, rather than deep in the economic underground, where it may run along, accumulating mass and speed, until it erupts unbidden and unheralded, a fully armed warrior of monetary chaos.

Consider: in recent years we have witnessed a fantastic growth in the popularity and prices of art works. And of real estate. And of common stocks. Coin collections, antiques, fine gems, rare books. Things that are widely believed to go up in money price over the years at least fast enough to preserve the purchasing power of the owners. Things which are, therefore, *substitutes for money*. In a long-term inflationary climate, such as the world has seen for the past three decades, money has been a very poor substitute for such *things*. Benjamin Anderson, I think, reminds us of the story of the two sons of an Austrian man who divided his wealth between them. One put his inheritance into a savings account; the other spent it on wine, which he consumed. After the great postwar inflation, the one who had the savings account was destitute, but the one who had a collection of empty wine bottles was slightly better off. The empty bottles sold for a larger quantity of schillings than there were in the original share of the inheritance.

Everyone knows the example of a man who took out a retirement-type insurance policy in the mid-1930s when $150 a month was enough to retire on. When he came to retire in 1960 he found that his money somehow didn't go so far as it used to or as he had thought it would. He had incurred a genuine and tangible loss, which he could trace back to the depreciation of the money. He may come to the conclusion that it had been an error in judgment to select the money system (an insurance policy funded upon fixed-interest government bonds) as a method of storing up value for the future. If a large enough number of people come to the conclusion that the money will not serve such a purpose, then the money system is at the brink of collapse. How close are we to that point? No one knows. Are we tending in that direction? I think so. Could the Coinage Act have stopped this trend? Yes.

The Coinage Act improved our small change system and got us started towards simplifying our money system, but it passed over a great opportunity to expand the usefulness of our money system. There is a world of reason to suspect that our money system is no longer serving one of the cardinal purposes of money, namely to store up value, and there was a simple way to get our money system started along the path towards that goal. At the very moment when we quite rightly removed intrinsic value from the small-change end of the money spectrum, we should have *added* a feature of intrinsic value to the long-range storehouse side of the money system. At the moment when we were untying the knots that bound our money to silver, we could have tightened and multiplied the connections between our money and gold.

It is strange that almost no one commented on this possibility. Yet gold as an alternative to silver seems like a very obvious idea. Silver must go, it was rightly said, because it is becoming an important industrial metal, and there isn't enough left over for coinage; whereas there is no need to coin gold, and there is plenty of gold in the world to serve as a monetary reserve. The trouble with silver is that it is mined as a by-product, and so its production does not respond to price movements—a very bad thing in a monetary metal; whereas gold is mined very much as a principal product, and gold production is quite sensitive to price movements. A money system tied to silver is at the mercy of wildly fluctuating price movements in the silver market (resulting from factors mentioned above); whereas the changes in the price of gold are small and tend to be gradual.

We could, I am saying, repeal the law that makes it a crime to own gold.

But that is quite another story indeed. Here I am concerned only to register a strong approval of the principal changes provided in the Coinage Act of 1965 and to raise a voice of regret that the Congress did not seize a grand opportunity to drive even further towards a truly useful and rational money system.

8. The Outlook

BY NOW IT should not be necessary to caution against an over-simple approach to the silver situation. A great number of forces are at work in the silver markets, and too many of them for comfort are inscrutable. The outlook is not knowable in detail therefore, but the general size and shape of things to come should be available to the patient student. It will be useful to look forward under the various aspects of the problem. The future of the U.S. coinage, U.S. prestige, the price of silver, the gold outflow, the prospect of controls, the opportunity for speculative profit—these are all bound up together.

The new cupronickel sandwich coins will be distributed in great quantities in 1966. Within three years the Mint should have produced enough of them to replace the previous silver coinage almost wholly. The cupronickel sandwiches will function satisfactorily as coins, but the chief question is what will happen to the silver coinage. Clearly the Treasury is counting on receiving a large quantity of silver from the return flow of silver coins—an expectation that I judge to be optimistic. As soon as the new sandwich coins have made their appearance around the country, an immense majority of the people will have the ancient monetary question laid plain before them: Do you prefer good money or bad? I see no reason why the American population will behave differently from other populations that have been placed in similar circumstances; indeed, there is more than a little evidence that the Americans have already begun to lay away the old, "good," "solid" coins. The prospect then must be for a vastly increased hoarding of silver coins after the sandwiches have made themselves sufficiently known. When will that be? I would set the date somewhere in the latter half of 1966. That is the time when a second sharp coin shortage should become manifest. However, it will be different from the great shortage of 1963-1964, because by this time the Government will have already adopted a program to alleviate it. From that point on, the problem of coin shortages should grow less and less serious until, by 1969, we will be up to our ears in cupro-nickel sandwiches, for what that's worth. No great long-lasting coin shortage in the immediate future; and a new coinage that will be useful for many decades; and the rather swift disappearance of all silver coins from visible circulation.

As to the prestige of the U.S., the question is not so hollow as it may sound. For many years the U.S. gold position has been terribly weak in relation to the short-term claims held by foreign central banks against our gold reserve. The main support in this situation has been U.S. prestige in the form of the myth that the biggest economy in the world will automatically guarantee the strongest currency in the world; and U.S. prestige in another sense, which is the prestige that it is in the interest of foreign central bankers to preserve by not starting a catastrophic run on the dollar (the idea that "we're all in this together"). Quite clearly the prestige of the U.S. is a function, over the long term, of the way in which the Federal Government manages the basic responsibilities of sovereignty. One of these is the regulation of the currency. In international matters the U.S. has not exactly covered itself with glory, unless one is to consider deficits glorious; if to this record we now add the disappearance of silver coinage at home, there is the outside chance that our foreign friends will tire of propping up the cadaver in the window. But only an outside chance, because it is clear that the troubles we are facing with the coinage are only partly the responsibility of the Treasury. The enormous alteration in the world supply and demand structure for silver has been of course beyond the control of any government. The Treasury should be castigated without mercy for its incompetent and dilatory response to the growing storm, but let us admit that the storm itself was not brewed in Washington. The chances are very good that the sophisticated men in charge of the principal central banks of Europe will not see in the disappearance of our silver coinage any sharp sign of imminent financial collapse.

What about the price of silver? There are few things in this life that are as certain as the outlook for this: the price of silver will go up. The only practical questions are when and by how much. If the Treasury has enough silver to hold the market price down to $1.29 during the transition to cupronickel sandwich, then the price won't start rising until 1969 or 1970. The Treasury probably can do that much. Starting with 800 million ounces at the end of 1965, the Treasury could supply 100 million ounces yearly to the world market in order to make up the difference between fresh production and industrial demand, and another 100 million ounces to bullion speculators (including corporate inventorying) yearly

—and thus hold the price for four years. At which time, assuming the Treasury had received no return flow of silver coins, its silver stock would be exhausted. However, as the point of exhaustion comes ever nearer, it is only reasonable to suspect that the pressures of anticipatory speculation will mount. (It is this kind of thing that produces the typical acceleration towards the end of major monetary movements.) If, allowing for this, we move the date forward a bit, we might hazard a very rough guess that the price of silver will start to move around mid-1968. It should be mentioned that the potential speculation will not be confined to the demand side of the market but will attract some votaries on the supply side also: that is, the producers of newly mined silver will tend to hold their new supplies off the market, allowing the U.S. Treasury to do the selling at $1.29, with the prospect of selling their own silver at higher prices once the Treasury has been cleaned out. Since the great bulk of silver production comes from foreign lands, it is easy to see that the U.S. Government will be able to exercise only the authority of diplomacy in this matter; diplomacy rarely conquers the forces of the market; the Treasury silver supplies will become the target of a worldwide raid.

As to the price of silver, one can do no better than to quote the Treasury Department itself, in its *Staff Study of Silver and Coinage* (p. 38):

A simple extension of the postwar trend of silver prices suggests that $2 an ounce might easily be reached by 1980 or 1985. Analysis of supply and demand factors does not yield any precise estimate of the level that silver prices might reach in a free market. The analysis does suggest that there is a very appreciable risk that price could reach $2 an ounce then, or even much sooner. Battelle's detailed quantitative projections of the rate of exhaustion of Treasury stocks lead to an even more pessimistic appraisal since with 50 per cent silver content they can foresee the complete exhaustion of Treasury silver as early as 1969.

This passage appeared in a summarizing section, and should be read with the understanding that it is an attempt to look on the brighter side of things. Earlier in that section of the report, the Treasury experts went into the question a little more deeply, and darkly (p. 36):

It is extremely doubtful whether recent experience offers any assurance whatsoever that silver prices would remain below $2 in the next two decades. Indeed, it is not at all difficult to contemplate the price rising much farther. It is very hard to rule out the possibility of a doubling or even a tripling in the price of silver unless it can be shown that a higher price of silver would cut back the consumption of silver appreciably from present levels.

"A simple extension" of the postwar price trend, as the Treasury says, would suggest a price of $2 by 1980. But to do this one must lay the pencil on the graph starting in 1945 and ending with the forcibly suppressed price of today. The most recent free-market experience with silver prices occurred between late 1961 (when the Treasury stopped selling free silver at 90¢) and mid-1963 (when the Treasury had to start supplying silver at $1.29). Lay the pencil along *that* portion of the graph, and you get a $2 price for silver before the year 1966 is out. All in all, I would be willing to guess that we shall see $2 silver before 1970, and that $2 should not be considered a stopping point.

The exhaustion of the Treasury stocks, the rise in the market price, and the disappearance of the silver coinage will go hand in hand. To quote the Treasury report once again (p. 37): "Indeed, once Treasury stocks were exhausted, the prospect of keeping any silver coinage in circulation would not be at all bright."

As to gold, I have already mentioned the psychological elements in the situation (the matter of "prestige"), and it remains only to ask whether the revolution in silver will cause any new burden on our balance of payments as a result of increased purchases abroad, or decreased sales, or both. In the absence of governmental intervention, the answer can only be that our balance of payments will show an initial benefit (as foreign buyers take unusual amounts of silver at the Treasury's giveaway price of $1.29) and a subsequent deterioration (as U.S. buyers turn to foreign sources once the Treasury has dried up, and pay $2 or more); it is well to recall that U.S. industry uses three times as much silver as is produced in the U.S. But the amount of silver that will be deflected in international trading is very small in comparison with the U.S. trade balance; it is nothing like the position of Zambian copper in the British economy. I would conclude that our revolution in silver will not cause any convulsions in our balance of payments or in our gold position—which is deteriorating on its own apparently inflexible schedule.

The prospect of governmental controls is a very real one. It will be recalled that the Roosevelt Administration completely hogtied the silver market and the silver producers in the 1930s as part of the general scheme to control the silver price (though no one has ever explained why the silver price had to be controlled). It is well established that, once the idea of governmental controls is accepted, there is no limit to their application. Thus if the Treasury seeks to avoid selling its silver stock to foreign buyers, it may ask for a law banning the export of silver. This being circumvented by sales for future delivery, a law must be written forbidding all silver dealings with foreigners. This being circumvented by silver dealings with U.S. corporations controlled by foreigners, a law must be written forbidding . . . etc. The whole subject was given extraordinary mention in the Treasury report—at the very end, of course, because official agencies avoid the mention of governmental coercion whenever they can. But there it was, on pages 88 and 89:

Brief comment will be made on the role that melting, hoarding, and export controls might play during the changeover to a base alloy, although full examination and analysis of the problem will not be attempted here. It may be desirable to obtain standby authority of the Secretary of the Treasury to institute controls over the hoarding, melting, and exporting of silver in the event he determines certain conditions occur. But, with the possible exception of export controls, the usefulness of such controls as part of an orderly changeover appears questionable; rather, their function would appear to be that of emergency maneuvers to be taken only if the possibility of holding the silver price through sales from our own stock during the critical changeover period is seriously threatened. If the changeover is started soon to a base alloy, this threat will undoubtedly be avoided.

The purpose to be served by controls over the melting of coin if the Treasury is able and willing to hold down the price of silver is questionable, since there would then be no incentive to melt coins. Furthermore, the prohibition of melting at the same time as the price of silver is being held could foster the misconception that the price was shortly going to be allowed to rise, and stimulate speculation in bullion.

Melting controls might be obligatory in a "last ditch" effort to maintain coin in circulation where the Treasury had tried to hold the price of silver, but then ran out of silver which could be sold in the market. In general, this would not even seem to be a remote possibility where the transition is to a base alloy, rather than to a reduced content silver alloy. Moreover, while melting controls could be required under some circumstances, too much should not be expected from their application, since a prohibition on melting could not effectively prevent hoarding under those circumstances.

Controls over the hoarding of coin, while perhaps conceivable in theory, would be extremely difficult to enforce effectively. It is hard to see just how controls could be designed which would discriminate successfully between prohibited hoarding and the accumulation of coin in the ordinary course of business, and in coin collections. Possibly, penalties for coin hoarding could be devised that would limit large accumulations by professional speculators, and such controls might play some part in effecting the recovery of old silver coin in the transition to silver coinage of reduced content. Even this seems doubtful, however, since a legal apparatus effective in dissipating large hoards would seem almost certain to encourage even more widespread "family" accumulations. While the question deserves fuller discussion and analysis than it will be given here, there does not seem to be much value in controls on the hoarding of coin. Controls on the hoarding of bullion might conceivably be more effective.

There is a stronger case for export controls during a changeover period. Certainly, they would be an essential backstop to any controls over the melting or hoarding of coin. But if these controls are not used because the Treasury is holding the market price of silver, the case for export controls on silver is much less clear.

The only situation in which we would want to prohibit the export of silver bullion would be during a period when there was heavy foreign speculative demand, which added to the drains on Treasury stock—as was the case temporarily in the latter months of 1964. However, one result of applying export controls would be a partial separation of the U.S. market from the world market, and there would be some increase in world prices above the pegged

U.S. price. As a consequence, some U.S. domestic demand for silver, previously met from imports, would now be met from Treasury stocks, a cheaper source of supply. By frustrating the foreign demand for Treasury silver, it could be argued that some net saving would arise. It should be recognized that silver users would probably regard the separation of U.S. and world markets as a threat to their assured sources of supply. If so, export controls might stimulate silver users to make precautionary purchases of Treasury silver in advance of their current requirements. The fact that, aside from speculative demands, the United States is a natural importer greatly increases the possibility of this response to a higher world price.

I cannot think of a comparable passage in the literature of bureaucracy. Here, in clear view, is the demon of centralized control. On point after point the authors of the Treasury report acknowledge that the introduction of one interventionary control must lead to the introduction of further controls, and will lead too often to results the opposite of those the government had intended in the first place.

Nevertheless, the report goes placidly on discussing the merits of this control and that; and we can be sure that the obvious lesson of the passage will not be learned. I find here the greatest single hazard in the silver revolution: the hazard of increased governmental intervention in private affairs. Even though it should be plain that the ultimate controls can never be effective (everyone in the land will have his $15 worth of silver coins), nevertheless the temptation to institute the very first control is always overpowering. Subsequent additional controls are defended not in their own right but on the grounds that they are merely supporting documents for the first control, which is already law, and so there is no disagreement about that, is there? And so on, until the economy loses great areas to the no-man's-land of political administration. The threat is as serious as it is real.

I come now to the question of the possibility of speculative opportunities in this period of monetary upheaval. It is axiomatic that speculative opportunities will arise in any period of rapidly changing prices, and it is all but absolutely certain that the price of silver must sooner or later come to rest at a level two or three times the present level. Already some handsome speculative profits have been recorded in the stock market: the common shares of silver mining companies have in some cases trebled in price over the last three years. Much of that rise may be attributed to the 42 per cent rise in the price of silver in the two years following November 1961. If a further and even greater rise in the price of silver may be foreseen over the next few years, then there would seem to be further opportunity for profit in silver mining stocks. It would be difficult for the government to write laws to expropriate such profits; consequently this opportunity seems real.

The bullion market seems less promising. Although it will reflect directly the rise in demand for silver, being the market in which silver prices are established, still the experience of recent years and the veiled remarks in the Treasury report are disquieting. Thirty years ago a special 50 per cent tax on profits made in silver bullion trading effectively closed the silver market in this country, and that demented law remained on the books until 1963; it is not as if we wouldn't do it again. The Treasury report speaks of "controls on the hoarding of bullion" in terms that betray a degree of confidence in their efficacy. No doubt the opportunity for profit in the bullion market is restricted mainly to the professional traders.

Simple coin hoarding, which appears to be going on at the moment, appears also to be the most reasonable route to profits in this period. There is, first, a good deal of mere keep-sake value in the "last real silver coins ever minted in this country." It is the kind of investment that can be undertaken by persons with limited capital: anyone with a dime can establish a speculative position in the silver coinage situation. The risk of loss is minimal. There is the assurance that a U.S. silver coin can always be exchanged for face value, and so the only exposure to loss would arise from misplacement, destruction, and interest forgone. As to the possibility that such hoarding might be declared illegal, the Treasury report speaks in unusually clear tones: "A legal apparatus effective in dissipating large hoards would seem almost certain to encourage even more widespread 'family' accumulations."

In this connection it is worth recalling that when the Roosevelt Administration made the holding of gold illegal, almost all of the gold stock was in the bank vaults anyway, with the result that the nationalization of gold did not involve writing a law that would make a criminal of every citizen in the land. With silver the situation is, of course, vastly different. Any law that makes it a crime to hold silver coins makes a criminal out of every citizen who handles money at all. The Treasury quite rightly says that there would be no way to halt the widespread accumulation of small holdings.

That a widespread accumulation is going on at the moment is suggested rather strongly by the figures on the return flow of silver coin to the banking system from individuals and businesses. In January of 1961, 1962, and 1963 the return flow averaged about $100 million. In January 1964 it was $78 million. In January 1965 it was $22 million—and this despite the immense minting under the Treasury's "crash" program! By the autumn of 1965 there were advertisements in the newspapers for silver coins *wanted* at a premium. One coin dealer offered 50.5¢ for any quantity of 50-cent pieces in any condition, but he probably didn't receive many at that price. Within six weeks he was offering 51.5¢ each, for any quantity of circulated halves. The half-dollars had been scarce for months beforehand, and the banking system was apparently cooperating in a quiet drive to recall all halves to Washington. The paymaster of one small business located in the East was told by his bank that he would get no more halves until the new coins were in circulation. So now the silver dollar, the Kennedy half, the Franklin half, and the Liberty half are apparently stashed away in private hoards. The game is getting rough.

By year-end 1965 there were about $2.7 billion of silver coin in circulation. The disappearance of the silver dollar and the half-dollar meant that $1.1 billion of silver coin had already been withdrawn from the transaction circuit. Assuming that no quarters and dimes had been hoarded as yet, there remained $829 million in silver quarters and $784 million in silver dimes doing business in the nation's tills and pockets. How long would this last, in a nation capable of soaking up $516 million worth of the Treasury's silver in 1965 alone? Any observer who has no inbuilt lust for chaos must hope that the Treasury spews out those cupronickel sandwiches with the speed of a short-order chef. Time is running out, and the silver with it.

Silver was never the backbone of our monetary system, but nevertheless in recent years it did serve in its minor fashion to measure the speed of our monetary debauch. Now it is gone, and the United States is on a completely fiat basis (the trivial connection between gold and that 20 per cent of our money supply that is composed of Federal Reserve notes can be, and will be, ignored). That is, for the first time since 1792, we are on a money backed by nothing better than the politician's pledge. The stage is set for the final inflationary blow-off if that is what our money managers desire. The shelves of the libraries groan under the weight of the evidence that wealth cannot be created through the printing of paper money, and the cemeteries are filled with the corpses of the grandees whose search for the philosopher's stone ended at the tomb. Our leaders have not learned from history. We cannot bid farewell to silver without profound foreboding.

Notes

CHAPTER 1

1. Federal Reserve Bank of New York, *Annual Report,* 1964, p. 48.
2. *Wall Street Journal,* June 8, 1964.
3. *Newsweek,* June 15, 1964.
4. *New York Times,* June 26, 1964.
5. *Federal Reserve Bulletin,* July 1964, p. 838.
6. *Wall Street Journal,* July 10, 1964.
7. *New York Herald Tribune,* January 24, 1965.
8. *Wall Street Journal,* August 24, 1964.
9. Publishers Newspaper Syndicate. *New York Herald Tribune,* November 16, 1964.
10. *New York Times,* December 22, 1964.
11. *New York Times,* January 13, 1965.
12. *Central Economic Letter,* Monthly Index of Business Activity for Cleveland and Northeast Ohio, published by Central National Bank of Cleveland, January 1965.
13. *Wall Street Journal,* February 10, 1965.
14. *Wall Street Journal,* ca. March 15, 1964.
15. *Wall Street Journal,* March 23, 1965.
16. *New York Times,* January 11, 1965.
17. *New York Times,* March 14, 1965.
18. *A Nation Without Coins,* by Charles R. Robinson and Charles B. Young (New York: Vantage Press, 1965), p. 16.
19. *Barron's,* April 19, 1965.

20. On May 30, 1814. *Jahrbuch der Goethe-Gesellschaft,* 1920, pp. 195-227. Cited in *The Numismatist,* December 1963, p. 1646.

21. Robinson and Young, op. cit., p. 17.

22. *New York Times,* May 8, 1964.

23. Treasury Department, Circulation Statement of United States Money, September 30, 1965.

24. For the early period in U.S. monetary history I have relied mainly on A. Barton Hepburn, *A History of Currency in the United States* (New York: Macmillan, 1915).

25. *Letters and Memoirs Relating to the War of American Independence,* by Madame de Riedesel (New York: G. & C. Carvill, 1827), p. 194. Riedesel Avenue, in Cambridge, Massachusetts, is named after the Baron and his family, who stayed there for a while after their capture before being sent to Warm Spring ("Bath"), Virginia, both because provisions were hard to come by up north, and because the Baron needed "the cure" on account of "sunstroke." See Mary C. Crawford, *The Romance of Old New England Rooftrees* (Boston: L. C. Page, 1903), p. 133. Perceval Reniers gives a delightful sketch of the Baroness in his elegant *The Springs of Virginia* (University of North Carolina Press, 1941).

26. These last few passages rely heavily on Dickson H. Leavens, *Silver Money* (Bloomington, Indiana: Principia Press, 1939).

CHAPTER 2

1. *Great River: The Rio Grande in North American History* (New York: Rinehart, 1954), I, p. 357.

2. The bulk of this section on the uses of silver relies upon Robinson and Young, op. cit., p. 30 ff. However, the current yearly consumption figures are different, resting as they do on later reports: a resume of 1964 by the Silver Users Association, 1625 Eye Street N.W., Washington, D.C.; and a speech given in New York City, March 18, 1965, by John B. Stevens, Vice President, International Silver Co.

3. Annual reports of Director of the Mint, quoted in Elgin Grose-close, *Silver and the Coinage Crisis,* 1964, a pamphlet issued by the Wall Street firm of Cyrus J. Lawrence & Sons (New York).

4. The Stevens source is noted in n. 2, above. Stevens was quoting an unidentified "statement by a Treasury official made on February 6."

5. "The Silver Market in 1964," 49th Annual Review, published by Handy & Harman, New York.

6. Robinson and Young, op. cit., p. 61, for data through 1950; Handy & Harman, op. cit., for data 1960 through 1964 (Free World only).

7. Robinson and Young, op. cit., p. 64.

8. Leavens, op. cit., p. 68.

CHAPTER 3

1. This sketch of the history of silver money is drawn largely from Hepburn, op. cit.; Anderson, op. cit.; Leavens, op. cit.; Elgin Groseclose, *Money and Man* (New York: Ungar, 1961); and Robinson and Young, op. cit.

2. Marija Gimbutas, *The Balts* (New York: Praeger, 1963).

3. Brooks Adams, *The Law of Civilization and Decay,* ch. 1.

4. Groseclose, *Money and Man,* p. 44.

5. The estimate is by William Jacob and is quoted in Leavens, op. cit., p. 2.

6. Adams, op. cit.

7. Anderson, op. cit., pp. 47-8.

CHAPTER 4

1. The figures can be derived by combining the production, consumption, and coinage figures given in 1) Groseclose, *Silver and the Coinage Crisis,* cited earlier, and 2) the *Invest-ment Bulletin,* June 15, 1964, of the American Institute for Economic Research.

2. Robinson and Young, op. cit., p. 101.

3. "Coin Shortage, Part I, Preceding Treasury's Crash Coin Production Program," *Sixth Report by the Committee on Government Operations,* House Report No. 194 (Washington, D.C.: March 22, 1965), pp. 15-19.
4. Reported in *Engineering & Mining Journal,* November 1961.
5. First National City Bank *Monthly Letter,* December 1961.
6. *Wall Street Journal,* Dec. 22, 1961. In this article the writer, Arlen Large, speaks of "some future Treasury Secretary" worrying about the silver question when it finally becomes acute "by the turn of the century." He means the year 2,000 A.D. The *WSJ* usually does better.
7. Not quite spring: March 11, 1963. Testimony before House Committee on Banking and Currency. Quoted in Robinson and Young, op. cit., p. 100.
8. *Wall Street Journal,* March 23, 1964.
9. *U.S. News & World Report,* July 27, 1964.
10. Quoted in *Federal Reserve Bulletin,* July 1964.
11. *Wall Street Journal,* August 12, 1964.
12. *New York Times,* September 16, 1964.
13. *New York Times,* October 3, 1964.
14. *New York Times,* October 15, 1964.
15. *New York Times,* October 21, 1964.
16. *Wall Street Journal,* December 15, 1964.
17. *New York Times,* May 4, 1965.

CHAPTER 5

1. The experience of other countries is drawn from Leavens, op. cit., pp. 153-162.
2. A public letter, May 12, 1965, from P. T. Noyes, President of the Sterling Silversmiths Guild of America, to Senator A. Willis Robertson, Chairman of the Banking and Currency Committee.
3. "Coin Shortage," op. cit., p. 8; and ibid., "Part II," *House Report No. 195,* p. 8 (Note).
4. A pictorial essay on coin-making appears in the *New York Times,* March 14, 1965, p. F-1.

5. See n. 3, above: *House Report No. 195,* pp. 26-27.
6. *Research Report,* June 14, 1965, of the American Institute for Economic Research (Great Barrington, Massachusetts).

CHAPTER 6

1. All references to the President's message may be checked by consulting the newspapers of June 4, or *House Document No. 199,* 89th Congress, 1st Session.
2. Groseclose, *Silver and the Coinage Crisis,* op. cit.; and Handy & Harman, *The Silver Market in 1964,* p. 19.
3. Groseclose, *Money and Man,* pp. 45-55.
4. *Wall Street Journal,* May 17, 1965.
5. *New York Times,* May 23, 1965.
6. *Wall Street Journal,* June 7, 1965.
7. *Wall Street Journal,* July 26, 1965.

CHAPTER 7

1. *Treasury Staff Study of Silver and Coinage,* 1965, p. 58.
2. *New York Post,* March 24, 1965.
3. Total money supply as defined and reported in *Federal Reserve Bulletin,* July 1965. Some economists—e.g., Melchior Palyi—include short-term U.S. Government paper in the money supply, arriving at totals in the neighborhood of $200 billion. As I say, "money" is an ill-defined term. The silver figures are from the June 30, 1965, "Circulation Statement of United States Money," issued by the Treasury Department; they include standard silver dollars, silver certificates, and subsidiary silver.

Glossary

Any special area of study will acquire a jargon, and there is no reason to avoid the jargon whenever it is accurate enough to be useful. For example, the jargon of sociology should be avoided because it is empty, refers to nothing distinct, and is often contradictory. But the jargon of economics hath its uses. Although I have made an attempt in the body of this book to use these terms in self-explanatory ways, I have not wanted to load the text with definitions. For easy reference, here are a few dozen of the shop-words that crop up most frequently in these pages.

arbitrage—the dealing in more than one market simultaneously, in order to take advantage of differences in price.

barter—any transaction in which commodities or manufactures are exchanged directly.

bimetallism—the monetary system in which the monetary unit is defined by law in terms of both gold and silver.

bullion—the monetary metal (gold or silver) in its uncoined state, whether bars or ingots or pellets; the pure metal.

bullion parity—the price of bullion at which the bullion contained in a coin is worth the face value of the coin.

cash—in business parlance, readily spendable assets, usually currency, checking accounts, short-term notes, and the like; in bank statements, currency alone.

circulation—currency (paper and coin) outside the vaults of the Federal Reserve banks; including hoards, vault cash.

coinage rate—under bimetallism, the ratio of silver to gold in the monetary unit.

coinage ratio—coinage rate.

coining value—the face value of coinage from a given quantity of bullion.

collector—anyone who stores up quantities of coin for instruction, amusement, or anticipated profit.

convertibility—ready exchangeability of a currency for another currency.

currency—tangible money; i.e., paper and coin.

demonetized—said of a metal, when the monetary unit is no longer defined in terms of it.

devaluation—redefinition of the monetary unit in terms of less metal or less foreign exchange than before.

elasticity—tendency of supply or demand to respond quickly and proportionately to changes in market prices.

étalon boiteux—the limping standard; said of a monetary system linked to a gold standard but retaining offsetting features such as non-redeemable silver, fiat currency, and the like.

face value—the money sum printed on a coin or a paper bill.

fiat money—the monetary unit not defined in terms of any metal or commodity.

fineness—proportion of gold or silver bullion, by weight, in alloyed bars or ingots or coins.

fractional notes—paper bills with a face value less than the monetary unit.

fractional pieces—subdivisions of an actual coin; specifically, the eight "bits" into which the Spanish Piece of Eight was commonly divided; giving rise to the expression still current, "two bits"—meaning two-eighths, or one-quarter, of a dollar.

free minting—the guarantee of the mint that it will turn into coinage any and all amounts of bullion brought to it; free in the sense of unlimited, but not in the sense of gratuitous: there may be a small minting charge.

free reserves—in recent U.S. history, the amount of silver bullion in the Treasury that was not held as legal backing for the silver certificates issued; arising from the difference between the market price of silver and its coining value.

free silver—in recent history, the free reserves.

grain—1/7000 pound avoirdupois.

Gresham's Law—the *tendency,* when two coins of equal face value but different intrinsic value are circulating together, for the one of lesser intrinsic value to remain in circulation and the one of greater intrinsic value to disappear from circulation.

hoarding—the storing up of coin with a view to profit.

inelasticity—tendency of supply and demand to respond sluggishly if at all to changes in market prices.

inflation—increase in the money supply disproportionately large in relation to increase in the monetary metal reserve or the increase in goods offered in the markets.

intrinsic value—the market value of the bullion content of coin.

legal ratio—coinage rate.

legal tender—whatever is declared by law to constitute satisfactory payment of debt; not all money is legal tender for all debts

—e.g., minor coin is legal tender for only the smallest obligations. (You cannot force a man to accept ten thousand pennies in payment of a $100 debt.)

melting point—bullion parity.

minor coin—our pennies and nickels.

mint rate—coinage rate.

mint ratio—coinage rate.

monetary unit—that form of money in terms of which all other forms are defined; the dollar in the U.S., in France the franc, etc.

monetary value—the bullion parity (= coining value).

monetization—the passage of metal (or any other good) into the monetary system so as to facilitate an increase in the money supply.

money—an inexact term; in general, anything that serves as a medium of exchange, standard of measurement, store of value, or means of deferred payment; in fiat phase, money is whatever the government says it is (whether paper, cardboard, wampum, or whatnot); in the present U.S. it includes a great variety of things (see "money supply").

money supply—in the present U.S., all gold and silver holdings of the government, plus currency, checking accounts, time deposits, and an indefinite amount of short-term debt instruments (mostly Treasury bills and notes).

nominal value—face value.

numismatics—the study of the history of coinages; often allied with the collection of examples of outstanding coinages; in any case the primary attraction is not pecuniary.

outstanding—when said of currency, the total issue believed to be extant outside the Treasury and the Mint.

redeemability—ready exchangeability of non-metallic forms of money for quantities of the monetary metal at a fixed rate.

scrip—fractional notes; paper bills, usually unsecured, of small denomination, and for temporary purposes.

seigniorage—a small minting charge (see "free minting"); more generally, the difference between the cost of the bullion content and the face value of coins minted.

speculator—anyone who buys and holds with an eye exclusively to selling at a profit.

sterling—silver alloy .925 fine.

subsidiary silver—our halves, quarters, and dimes before the Coinage Act of 1965; during the transaction to the new coinage, the term will be ambiguous; after the new coinage is entirely established, "subsidiary silver" will refer only to the new 40 per cent silver Kennedy half.

troy ounce—480 grains.

Appendix: Extracts from *Treasury Staff Study of Silver and Coinage*

[IV.]
Metallurgical and Technical Characteristics of Alternative Coinage Alloys

This section...is concerned with the metallurgical and technical characteristics of the various coinage alloys that might replace silver of 900 fineness in a new coinage system....

The analysis of the preceding section has led to the elimination of silver alloys of more than 500 fineness because of the prohibitive risk that the market price of silver would reach, or exceed, $2 an ounce within the next 20 years or so....

Aluminum

Public Acceptability

Aluminum coins are unlikely to be acceptable to the public. Pure aluminum is very light in weight with a density of 2.7 grams per cubic centimeter, in contrast to a density of 10.3 for 900 fine silver. Aluminum is also very soft. It could be hardened by the addition of manganese but its wearing qualities would still be relatively poor. Aluminum can be processed so as to produce different colored coins but this seems unlikely to increase its chances for public acceptance. Foreign coinage use of aluminum is chiefly limited to low denominations. There are some examples of use by developed industrial countries; namely, Austria, Italy, and Japan. On balance, it would seem that aluminum would be rated very low in acceptability by the public if proposed as the basic alloy in a new coinage system. It is conceivable that an aluminum 1-cent piece would be acceptable to the public, but its use in high denominations lacks precedent elsewhere and probably would encounter strong public opposition.

Operation in Vending Machines

Pure aluminum has an electrical resistivity of about 2.7 microhms-cm. This is close to the 2.1 resistivity of 900 fine silver and the 3.1 of the present 1-cent piece. However, current vending machines depend not only upon coins being nonmagnetic, of proper size, and of appropriate electrical resistivity; they also depend upon coins being of a certain minimum weight in order to roll properly and they use a bounce test for hardness.[1] Aluminum coins fall below minimum weight requirements and existing vending machine rejectors cannot easily be redesignated to handle lightweight coins. Furthermore, if manganese were added in order to harden aluminum coins, their electrical resistivity would be raised well above that of the present 1-, 10-, 25-, and 50-cent pieces. Undoubtedly, some rejection apparatus could eventually be designed to take aluminum coins and reject other alloys. No such apparatus is available now and no one is known to be working on the problem.

Counterfeiting Potential

Unless aluminum coins were to receive some special processing, the potential for counterfeiting would seem to be very great. Sheet aluminum is readily available and the manufacture of coin

[1]The best single parameter in this connection is probably the product of an alloy's electrical resistivity and its density. Throughout most of the ensuing discussion that deals with vending machine operation, attention is confined to electrical resistivity because the densities of eligible coinage alloys do not vary widely.

blanks would not be difficult at all. The metal is soft and would take impressions readily from counterfeit dies. If the dies were of high quality, the minting of aluminum counterfeits might become a problem of some proportions.

Aside from the threat of direct counterfeiting, aluminum blanks would probably pose a real problem for the vending machine industry. Rejectors might eventually have to be equipped with some sensing device by which blanks could be told from coins. This would undoubtedly prove to be difficult and expensive.

Ease and Certainty of Production

Aluminum is a very easy material to work and over the long run it probably would not present any difficult minting problems. The Mint has had no production experience working with aluminum, but experimentally it has been established that present techniques could be adapted readily to the fabrication of any material as soft as aluminum.

Cost and Availability of Raw Materials

Aluminum is cheap with a domestic market price of 24½ cents per pound for unalloyed primary aluminum ingot. Mint requirements would be tiny in proportion to U.S. annual consumption of aluminum of some 3 million short tons.

Conclusion: Rejected as possible coinage alloy.

Reasons: Lack of public acceptability, vending machine, and counterfeiting problems.

Columbium

Public Acceptability

Columbium has been proposed as a coinage material in the 50-cent piece and as a cladding material. The density of columbium is 8.57, just a little less than copper (8.96) and nickel (8.90). The color is gray, the ring is about the same as with silver, and the material is tarnish resistant. Wearing qualities should be appreciably better than those of silver coins. Public acceptability, as with any "exotic" material, is somewhat uncertain.

Operation in Vending Machines

Very little work has been done on the adaptation of vending machine rejectors that would be required with a pure columbium coin, or a columbium alloy. In theory, there would not appear to be any insuperable difficulties but practical experience is lacking. Columbium is fairly heavy and it is nonmagnetic. Its electrical resistivity is in the range of 12.5 to 16.0 microhms-cm, depending upon temperature. This compares with an average resistivity of 2.1 for 900 fine silver and 32.0 for cupronickel (the alloy in the 5-cent piece).

There have been experiments with powder metallurgy techniques in an effort to develop a columbium alloy which would work in existing vending machine rejectors without any alteration being required. However, at the time of writing, these efforts had not progressed much beyond the experimental stage and had not achieved the required degree of success under operating conditions.

Counterfeiting Potential

Columbium coins would be very difficult to imitate with any material of relatively low value.

Ease and Certainty of Production

The melting point of columbium is exceptionally high—4,474° F. to silver's 1,760° F. Columbium strip would have to be purchased from suppliers, or the Mint would have to acquire new equipment. It is said to be a very ductile material which does not work-harden when cold fabricated. The Mint should be able to make coins from purchased strip of columbium, although costs of fabrication would be somewhat greater.

Cost and Availability of Raw Materials

While fairly acceptable from other points of view, the cost of columbium is prohibitive. A price of $20 to $35 an avoirdupois pound was initially mentioned to the Treasury but a price range of $36 to $50 is quoted in the *American Metal Market*. Even the $20 to $35 price is well above a current price of $18.81 for silver. It is conceivable that on a large guaranteed coinage demand, unit costs might be reduced to, or below, $10 a pound. This would still be a very expensive coinage material.

There has been no U.S. mine production of columbium ore in recent years. About 60 percent of U.S. imports of columbium concentrate are from Canada; the rest are rather widely dispersed. Domestic stocks of concentrate and ingot are fairly sizable relative to demand for the metal but it is estimated by Battelle that it would take 2 to 3 years to expand production appreciably. Furthermore, coinage requirements would apparently be very large relative to current consumption of the metal and large relative to the national (strategic) stockpile.

Conclusion: Rejected as possible coinage alloy.

Reasons: High cost and uncertain supply outlook. Not accepted in present vending machines. Mint cannot fabricate with existing equipment.

75 Copper-25 Nickel (Cupronickel)

Public Acceptability

Cupronickel is the alloy presently used in the U.S. 5-cent piece and the most widely used coinage material in the world. The weight is good with a density of about 8.6 in contrast to a density of 10.3 for 900 fine silver, and about 9.6 for 500 fine silver. A cupronickel 25-cent piece would weigh 5.37 grams in contrast to 5.83 grams for 500 fine silver, and 6.25 grams for the present 900 fine 25-cent piece. The color is very good. Cupronickel does lack the luster of coin silver when the silver is untarnished. Also, its ring is not quite so impressive as that of the existing silver coins. However, a cupronickel coin ages well and its physical wear characteristics are very good—appreciably better than those of silver.

Cupronickel coinage has been used for relatively high denomination coins in the United Kingdom and has circulated side by side with silver coinage. Some objection to the use of cupronickel here would be lodged by individuals and groups who, for one reason or another, favor coinage with high intrinsic value. However, this sort of objection would be encountered if any base alloy were proposed for use in the 10-, 25-, and 50-cent pieces. It should be countered by insistence that under modern conditions high intrinsic value in subsidiary coinage tends to interfere with, rather than facilitate, performance of the essential medium of exchange function.

A question arises as to the role of the present 5-cent piece in a cupronickel system. Continuation of the 5- and 10-cent pieces in their present size and diameter, which probably is desirable, would lead to the anomaly of a 5-cent piece larger than the 10-cent piece, but made from exactly the same material. Opinions will differ as to whether this is important, but it is possible that some other material should be used for the 5-cent piece if cupronickel were to be used in the subsidiary denominations.

Operation in Vending Machines

Cupronickel has a resistivity of 32.0 microhms-cm, which is well above the 2.1 resistivity of 900 fine silver. Because existing rejectors are constructed to accept cupronickel 5-cent pieces, no unusually difficult problems are encountered in making a rejector that will accept cupronickel subsidiary coinage along with silver subsidiary coinage....

Counterfeiting Potential

The direct counterfeiting potential with cupronickel coinage should be quite low. Despite its comparative cheapness, cupronickel is not readily available from commercial suppliers. There are vending machine problems with a proposed subsidiary cupronickel coinage, but they relate to the use of foreign coins, or expanded U.S. 5-cent coins. The problem, in the instance of vending machines, is not so much the potential use of blanks, for they would be relatively difficult to obtain.

The rejector industry representatives do anticipate that a problem would arise if the U.S. were to switch to cupronickel subsidiary coinage, because of the use in vending machines of low-value foreign coins made from cupronickel. They have furnished a lengthy list of these coins which are sufficiently close in size to the U.S. 25-cent piece to operate a rejector mechanism set for a U.S. cupronickel 25-cent piece.

In addition, there is a potential problem with a cupronickel system in that the 5-cent piece could be flattened in a hydraulic press or by some other means and used as a 25-cent piece. Whether or not this would occur on any significant scale is questionable, but it is a further minor difficulty with a cupronickel system. This particular difficulty would not be overcome by substituting a 5-cent piece made of nickel silver in the cupronickel series since the two alloys have similar electrical resistivity.

Ease and Certainty of Production

The Mint has had long experience with the fabrication and minting of cupronickel. This is an important consideration where large numbers of coins may have to be produced in a very short period of time. Cupronickel is a tougher material than silver and is not quite so easy to mint. However, no unusual problems would be encountered and cupronickel must be rated very high in terms of ease and certainty of production.

Cost and Availability of Raw Materials

Cupronickel is also very attractive from the standpoint of the cost and availability of raw materials. Copper at 33 cents a pound and nickel at 79 cents a pound—alloy cost 45 cents—would be used in place of silver at $18.81 a pound. Coinage at the projected fiscal 1965 rate would use approximately 5,355 short tons of copper and 1,785 short tons of nickel annually. Copper presents no serious supply problem on a long-run basis, although intermittent shortages and sharp price movements can be expected to occur at times. Coinage needs would be a very small fraction of total consumption. The annual amounts of nickel used would be very small relative to U.S. consumption of 124,500 short tons in 1963.

Conclusion: Acceptable as coinage alloy.

Copper-Zinc Alloy (98 Copper-2 Zinc)

This alloy is red in color and its use for higher denomination coins does not merit any extended discussion. Along with similar alloys such as 96 copper-4 nickel, it does have an electrical resistivity similar to that of silver and could be used in existing rejectors. Some rejectors, which have been set specifically to reject copper slugs and cut-down pennies, would require minor adjustment. Copper-zinc coins could be easily fabricated on existing and planned Mint equipment. Because of their red color, they would merit consideration chiefly as an emergency measure, if silver were not available for coinage, and necessary vending machine adjustments were not yet complete. It is also conceivable that such an alloy might be used for the 5-cent piece if cupronickel were used for subsidiary coinage.

Nickel (Pure)

Public Acceptability

Pure nickel has a density of 8.90, approximately the same as cupronickel. It is whitish-gray in color and in mint condition is generally considered to be slightly more attractive than a cupronickel coin. Wearing qualities are excellent. Nickel is being more and more widely used as a coinage material although often a silver coin of higher denomination is retained in the series. This has been the case in Switzerland, Canada, France, the Netherlands, and Japan. South Africa has recently announced plans to replace its existing subsidiary coinage of 500 fine silver (reduced from 800 fine in 1951) with pure nickel coins, while retaining one high-denomination silver coin. Pure nickel coins would probably be readily accepted by the American public. The coins are very attractive and more closely resemble silver coinage than is the case with any of the base alloys, except nickel silver when it is in mint condition.

Operation in Vending Machines

Pure nickel is magnetic and existing rejector mechanisms are designed so as not to accept coins which are magnetic. It would be necessary entirely to redesign rejector mechanisms so as to be able to pass magnetic nickel coins but to reject magnetic iron slugs. While this probably could be done, it would be very difficult and could not be done quickly, particularly since practically all coin-operated mechanisms now depend upon the magnetic principle to some extent, and many less sophisticated mechanisms depend upon it entirely....

Counterfeiting Potential

Pure nickel coins would be extremely difficult to counterfeit because of the metal's relatively high melting point (2651° F.) and its hardness. There is little basis upon which to assess the potential for the use of nickel blanks, or blanks with comparable electrical resistivity, in vending machines since it is not clear what sort of rejector could be designed to accept pure nickel coins. The electrical resistivity of pure nickel is 9.5 microhms-cm. No other commonly used coinage alloy has a resistivity very close to that value although many brasses and bronzes, available commercially, do have similar resistivities.

Ease and Certainty of Production

Production of pure nickel coins would pose a very difficult problem for the Mint. Existing brass mill equipment could not be used because of the high melting point of nickel. The new Mint would have to be specially designed and/or nickel strip would have to be purchased for use in existing Mint facilities. The minting of nickel coins would still be very difficult with existing equipment even if strip were purchased, but it could be accomplished.

Cost and Availability of Raw Materials

Nickel costs 79 cents per pound. The International Nickel Company has estimated that at fiscal year 1965's projected rate of production of 10-, 25-, and 50-cent pieces about 15.7 million pounds of nickel would be required. These requirements would have to be met by imports from Canada or from the domestic stockpile. U.S. mine output comes exclusively from the Hanna Mining Company's properties in Oregon. In 1963, the nickel content of Hanna's production of ferronickel was about 21.4 million pounds but this ferronickel would not be suitable for mint requirements.

Conclusion: Rejected as possible coinage alloy.

Reasons: Vending machine problem associated with use of a magnetic alloy. Otherwise acceptable, although difficult to make with existing Mint equipment.

Nickel (Inco Alloy 95–Nickel 5–Silicon)

The International Nickel Company has developed an alloy of 95 nickel and 5 silicon which is nonmagnetic, thus removing, at least potentially, the major barrier to the use of nickel in slug rejectors of the present type. A further effort has been made to modify the alloy so that it will simulate the properties of 900 fine silver coinage and work in unaltered coin rejectors.

As one of their tests, existing rejectors roll the coin through a magnetic field. A coinage metal such as silver with very low electrical resistivity is slowed more in its travel, by eddy currents induced as it passes through the magnetic field, than is a material of higher electrical resistivity. Silver is a relatively "slow" coin, while cupronickel, for example, is a relatively "fast" coin. Having removed the magnetism of pure nickel coinage through the addition of 5 percent silicon, Inco technicians have sought to restore just such a sufficient degree of weak magnetism to the coin as to make it as "slow" as silver. In their most successful effort, the weak magnetism pulls the coin into contact with a piece of aluminum oxide tape which retards the rolling coin through physical friction. Without this retardation the 95-nickel 5-silicon coin would be too fast, since its electrical resistivity is higher than that of silver coins. The required magnetism has been sought at various times by adding a thin core of pure nickel, or a core of 80 percent nickel and 20 percent iron to the coin. The 80 percent nickel and 20 percent iron core is now preferred since its magnetism does not vary within the ranges of temperature that would be encountered....

Aside from the technical issue of use in vending machines, comment on the modified nickel coin can be relatively brief since many general comments applicable to pure nickel coinage are also applicable here.

Public Acceptability

The public would seem likely to accept the modified coin about as readily as a pure nickel coin.

Operation in Vending Machines

Discussed above.

Counterfeiting Potential

This would be a very difficult coin to counterfeit, at least as difficult as a pure nickel coin, and probably more difficult. . . .

Ease and Certainty of Production

It is very doubtful whether the Mint could make the modified nickel alloy; certainly it would be an expensive undertaking requiring different equipment. The necessary facilities could probably be included in the new Philadelphia Mint. If the modified alloy were to be used it apparently would be necessary to buy annealed blanks from Inco, at least until the new Mint is on stream. It is possible that current and planned rates of subsidiary coin production could be achieved using the purchased blanks. . . .

Cost and Availability

Inco has estimated that the coiled strip would cost $1.50 per pound; this includes a metal cost of about 80 cents per pound. The coinage requirements for nickel have been discussed above. At the fiscal 1965 rate, about 15.7 million pounds would be needed, roughly 6 percent of U.S. annual nickel consumption. The overall supply situation is probably adequate. . . .

The Bureau of Mines estimates known Canadian nickel reserves at 6 million tons and describes this as a very conservative appraisal. Canada is the principal Free World supplier of nickel and has accounted for about 80 percent of Free World production in recent years, and has supplied almost all of U.S. import requirements. Free World production of nickel was some 270,000 tons in 1963; almost half of this was consumed in the United States. If Free World consumption continued at the 1963 rate, known Canadian reserves would be depleted in about 25 years. Very large nickel reserves exist in New Caledonia and Cuba; but these should be excluded in determining the adequacy of nickel supply.

Nickel prices have almost tripled during the postwar period. Market shortages do not now exist but it cannot be said with complete assurance that they could not arise within, say, 20 to 25 years....

> Conclusion: Acceptable coinage alloy if consistent operation in vending machines could be demonstrated under operating conditions. Could not be fabricated on existing Mint equipment but coins could be struck at the Mint from annealed blanks.

Nickel Silver (65 Copper–18 Nickel–17 Zinc)

Public Acceptability

Also termed German silver, this alloy differs from cupronickel by the substitution of zinc for some nickel and copper. Proportions can vary but the 65 copper, 18 nickel, and 17 zinc alloy is probably best suited for coinage use. Because the alloy is fairly close in metallurgical composition and other characteristics to cupronickel, its advantages and disadvantages are perhaps best established by direct comparison with cupronickel, where that is possible. Nickel silver is slightly lower in weight than cupronickel because some zinc with a density of 7.1 is substituted for nickel and copper with densities of 8.9. When newly minted, the coin is very attractive and has a silverlike appearance, but it develops a yellowish cast as it tarnishes with age, while cupronickel keeps its grayish-white color indefinitely. Wearing qualities of nickel silver are also somewhat inferior to those of cupronickel; the ring of the two coins is similar. Nickel silver is not very widely used for coinage. Some current examples are Portugal, Philippines, and Taiwan.

In general, nickel silver must be rated a little below cupronickel in most of the characteristics that would be likely to influence public acceptability. The margin of superiority for cupronickel is not extremely wide but it is consistent. Public acceptability of nickel silver might conceivably be affected adversely by the fact that it is a rather cheap silver substitute with extensive household uses, *e.g.*, it is the common base for silver-plated flatware.

Operation in Vending Machines

The electrical resistivities of nickel silver (29.0) and cupronickel (32.0) are close, both are nonmagnetic and would have similar roll properties. Nickel silver coins of the right size will work in existing rejector apparatus set for the cupronickel 5-cent piece. As noted previously, this opens the possibility of making the 5-cent piece in a new system from nickel silver and making 10-, 25-, and 50-cent pieces from cupronickel. From the standpoint of minimizing the vending machine adjustment problem another possibility would be to leave the current 5-cent piece unchanged and to introduce nickel silver 10-, 25-, and 50-cent pieces. Either system would work in the prototype NRCO Model X rejector along with existing coinage. Either system, or ones exclusively of cupronickel or nickel silver, would have a 5-cent piece that could be flattened to work as a quarter in vending machines.

Counterfeiting Potential

Nickel silver would offer slightly more potential for counterfeiting than would cupronickel. Both are relatively cheap materials but nickel silver is much more readily available from a wide range of commercial suppliers. The same consideration suggests that the use of nickel silver blanks in vending machines would be more likely than cupronickel. Although the use of nickel silver blanks in the 5-cent slots of existing rejectors has not been brought to the Treasury's attention, it is possible that a problem might develop if a new system were to use nickel silver in the higher denominations.

Ease and Certainty of Production

The Mint has made nickel silver coins for foreign countries and the experience was satisfactory. The melting of the alloy materials produces zinc fumes which could be a problem where Mint facilities are located in downtown regions. The fumes can be removed by the installation and operation of electrostatic precipitators, or the copper and zinc can be prealloyed in a separate melting operation. The resulting increase in cost can be estimated at roughly 10 percent....

Cost and Availability of Raw Materials

Manufacturing costs would be somewhat higher on this alloy than on cupronickel although materials cost would be slightly lower since some zinc is substituted for copper and nickel. Zinc is only about one-sixth as expensive as nickel, and ordinarily about one-third to one-half as expensive as copper. The overall difference in cost between cupronickel and nickel silver alloys would not be large enough to influence the choice between them.

Conclusion: Acceptable as possible coinage alloy.

Plastic Coinage

Several exploratory letters have been written to the Treasury by firms engaged in the manufacture of plastics. One firm sent a sample plastic medallion to the Treasury, but the overall appearance of the medallion did not inspire confidence as to the degree of public acceptability plastic coinage would find. It is possible that in time some combination of powdered metal and plastics technology could be used to produce satisfactory coins. However, the Treasury has no reason to believe that such developments are imminent. The case for the introduction of plastic coins was argued by the Comptroller of the Royal Mint several years ago. At the time this aroused some interest in plastic as a coinage material. This interest seems now to have ebbed. There are no known instances of the use of plastic as a coinage material, and it must be rejected from consideration on the basis of the present technology. Much the same verdict must be given on glass coins.

Conclusion: Rejected—poor quality and probable public aversion to nonmetallic coins.

Stainless Steel

Public Acceptability

Stainless steel is lighter than most of the conventional coinage materials with a density of about 7.8 to 8.0 depending upon its composition. Coins made of stainless steel are white in color and their wearing qualities are superior to those of any other coinage material, except possibly pure nickel coins. Because stainless steel is very hard, coins have to be made with less relief, *i.e.,* the design and lettering are not raised as far from the coin background as in the case of coins made from softer alloys. The overall appearance of stainless steel coins suffers as a consequence....

Plain carbon steel can be clad with a relatively thin layer of another material, usually about 15 percent of the thickness on each side. Cladding materials currently being used in this way are nickel and cupronickel in Argentina, brass and copper in West Germany. The edges of these coins are unattractive and susceptible to rust....

Operation in Vending Machines

Vending machine test results on stainless steel have not been encouraging to date. Stainless steels containing 10 percent and more of nickel are nonmagnetic in their unworked state. But, a major difficulty is that so-called nonmagnetic stainless steels become magnetic when cold-worked, and the coins would then be rejected in vending machines. Three types of stainless steel, presumably nonmagnetic, were supplied for rejector tests. Blanks made from each of the three types of steel were refused by the rejectors. These blanks had been upset at the Mint before testing and even this small amount of fabrication was apparently sufficient to induce some magnetism. The actual stamping process might well have an even stronger effect upon stainless steel blanks. It may be that some stainless steel, suitable for coinage, can be found that will remain nonmagnetic....

Counterfeiting Potential

Actual duplication of a stainless steel coin would be a very difficult task because of the hardness of stainless steel. Although direct counterfeiting would probably not constitute a serious problem because coins would be so difficult to mint, the use of stainless steel blanks in vending machines would seem to pose a threat of some consequence....

Ease and Certainty of Production

Stainless steel presents serious problems for the Mint. It would be necessary, pending the construction of necessary facilities, to purchase the stainless steel from outside suppliers in the form of strip. Even so, the methods of coin fabrication would be entirely different from those used in the past, or those that are presently contemplated for the new Mint. It is true that the Mint made some magnetic stainless steel coins for Costa Rica but only with great difficulty. Mint experience on that production established that entirely new fabrication techniques would be required for coins larger than the U.S. 25-cent piece.

Conclusion: Rejected as possible coinage alloy.

Reasons: Some question as to public acceptability, replacement of existing vending machine rejectors, and difficult production problems.

Silver (500 Silver—500 Copper)

Public Acceptability

Silver coins of 500 fineness would be slightly lighter than existing coins because the density of copper is less than that of silver. The present 50-cent piece weighs 12.50 grams; a silver 50-cent piece of 500 silver and 500 copper would weigh 11.66 grams. It would be possible to tell 500 fine coins from 900 fine coins simply by weighing the coins in question.

Newly minted 500 fine silver coins could be made to resemble existing silver coins by being given an acid bath at a final production stage. This bath etches away the copper from the surface of the coin, leaving a thin film of silver. With wear, now intensified by the use of coins in vending machines which test for size, the external film of silver is rubbed off. This exposes reddish and yellowish areas on the coin and gives it an unattractive mottled appearance.

Largely because of these poor wearing qualities, 500 silver-500 copper is not generally considered to be an acceptable coinage alloy. The last country using 500 silver-500 copper is South Africa which has recently announced its decision to replace the 500 alloy with pure nickel coins.

Public acceptability of a 500 silver-500 copper coin is highly questionable.

Operation in Vending Machines

A strong point with 500 silver-500 copper coinage is the very minor adjustment of vending machine rejectors that would be required. The slight change in weight and electrical resistivity from existing silver coinage would not affect the majority of vending machines at all....

Counterfeiting Potential

There probably would be no serious increase in counterfeiting potential with the 500 silver-500 copper coinage, at first. As worn 500 fine coins began to make up the bulk of coins in circulation, some wider latitude for counterfeit coins would begin to emerge to the extent that the worn 500 fine coins would be less readily distinguished than the present coinage from cheap imitations made from base metals....

Ease and Certainty of Production

It is estimated that the use of an acid bath treatment to improve the initial appearance of the coins would increase current Mint operating costs by about 10 percent. In addition, new equipment and additional space would be required which the Mint does not have at present.

Cost and Availability of Raw Materials

The reduction of silver content from 900 to 500 fineness would reduce the direct cost of coinage metal by more than 40 percent for a given level of silver prices. Questions of the availability of raw materials are complex and center upon the adequacy of Treasury silver stocks to meet future coinage demand, without recourse to market purchases. These questions are discussed subsequently.

Conclusion: Rejected.

Reasons: Very poor appearance when worn. A quaternary silver, discussed next, is preferred on the basis of wear characteristics. A clad silver coin, subsequently discussed, would have the desirable vending machine properties of 500 silver-500 copper.

Silver Alloy—United Kingdom (500 Silver—400 Copper— 50 Nickel—50 Zinc)

Public Acceptability

The United Kingdom and a large number of other countries have in the past used an alloy consisting of 500 silver, 400 copper, 50 nickel, and 50 zinc. Sweden coins an alloy of 400 silver, 500 copper, 50 nickel, and 50 zinc; Finland, one of 350 silver, 570 copper, and 80 zinc; and Mexico one of 100 silver, 700 copper, 100 nickel, and 100 zinc. The addition of nickel and zinc to low silver content alloys reduces the rate of deterioration in appearance. When newly minted the coins, and even those of lower fineness than 500, are relatively attractive. However, the appearance of circulated coins would still leave much to be desired, despite the addition of nickel and zinc that helps to delay the appearance of the mottled surface that is characteristic of coins of low silver content. On technical and metallurgical grounds, the 500 quaternary alloy is not acceptable if coins are required to wear well and retain their appearance for 20 to 25 years. Consequently, it is clear that the alloy merits consideration only if a very high premium is placed upon the retention of some silver in the coinage. Even then, in the judgment of the Mint technical staff, the quaternary alloys would be a poor way to accomplish this end. Silver clad coins with high content silver as the outside layers would be preferable on the grounds of appearance and wear characteristics.

Operation in Vending Machines and Counterfeiting Potential

The addition of nickel and zinc in the quaternary alloy raises the electrical resistivity of the hardened coin to about 6.8 microhms-cm. This means that the coins would not work in vending machines with the eddy-current rejector. The resistivity range of rejectors could probably be widened to accept the existing coinage and the quaternary alloy but this would be a major undertaking, involving major revamping or replacement. Furthermore, if this were done, vending machines would be much more vulnerable to a variety of foreign coins and blanks than they are at the present time. The potential for direct counterfeiting of this alloy would not differ greatly from that for 500 silver-500 copper.

Ease and Certainty of Production

A quaternary alloy is a much more difficult problem for the Mint but it could be made without drastic change in existing procedures and equipment....

Cost and Availability of Raw Materials

As in the case of 500 silver-500 copper, the major uncertainty is the price and availability of silver in the event that Treasury stocks did not prove adequate to meet coinage and other requirements.

Conclusion: Barely acceptable as a coinage alloy.

Silver Clad Coins

Battelle has examined a wide range of multilayered coinage materials, including some with high-content silver alloys as the outside layers. The inner core on these coins could either be pure copper or a low-content silver-copper alloy with the overall fineness of the alloy varying according to the exact specifications of the outside layers and the inner core. If the present 900 fineness alloy were to be clad on a pure copper core, the resulting material would be approximately 400 in fineness. Much the same overall fineness could be achieved by using 800 fineness silver as the outside cladding and substituting a low-content silver-copper alloy as the inner core. For example, the Mint has made experimental strikes from 800 fineness silver clad on a 215 fineness silver-copper core which gives an overall fineness of 400.

The requirement of a minimum thickness of cladding to insure reasonable wear characteristics precludes any marked reduction in overall silver content and for practical purposes an average fineness of 400 can be taken as broadly representative of the minimum silver content, acceptable from a technical and metallurgical standpoint, where high fineness silver is clad on a pure copper or a low-content silver core. Any fineness much lower than 800 in the outside cladding would not make an acceptable coin.[1]

Public Acceptability

Silver-clad coins would be quite attractive in appearance if the outside cladding were at least 800 fineness. In such a case, the color would be the same as that of the present silver coinage except on the edges of the coins. When the core is composed of silver-copper alloy the edges of newly minted coins differ very slightly from the present coinage. Wear characteristics of silver-clad coins would be satisfactory if minimum thickness requirements were observed on the outside cladding.

Operation in Vending Machines

The high silver-copper clad on low silver-copper alloys would work in all vending machines without adjustment. If a pure copper core were used, most machines would need adjustment and pure copper slugs would then be accepted.

---

[1] On the basis of their analysis of the overall silver situation, Battelle determined that it would probably be necessary to reduce the silver content of the coinage to about 15 percent, and even so the need might arise to abandon silver altogether as a coinage material sometime in the 1970's. Consequently, their primary recommendations were for base alloy coinage, but they also suggested that if any silver were to be retained in the subsidiary coinage, it should either be limited to a high-content half-dollar or spread very thinly through the subsidiary coinage. In the latter case, they suggested that a 400 fineness silver quaternary alloy used as outside cladding on a copper-alloy core "might possibly meet minimum standards of acceptable appearance." In the judgment of the Mint technical staff, the quaternary silver alloys are undesirable on technical and metallurgical grounds and the exterior silver cladding on any composite coin should not be reduced below 800.

Counterfeiting Potential

Clad coins would be more difficult to counterfeit than the existing silver coinage.

Ease and Certainty of Production

The Mint has a substantial but limited capacity for the melting and rolling of silver-copper alloy strips but would probably have to purchase strip from outside suppliers. As a general proposition, it appears that the cladding of silver would present some difficulties where dependence had to be placed upon outside suppliers for a large volume of material. In any event, all bonding (cladding) operations would have to be performed in private plants.

Cost and Availability of Raw Materials

As with coinage of 500 fineness, the crucial question is whether Treasury stocks of silver would be adequate to meet long-run coinage requirements, and, if not, what effect Treasury purchases of silver in the market would have upon price.

Conclusion: Acceptable coinage alloy from a technical and metallurgical point of view.

Other Clad Coins: Cupronickel (or Nickel-Silver) Clad on a Copper Core

The multilayer principle recommended by Battelle can be applied to base alloy coinage. Coins with outer layers of cupronickel clad on a copper core will operate in existing vending machine rejectors along with the present silver coinage (probably nickel-silver would also work as outside cladding but tests have not been made). This resolution of the vending machine problem would allow the rapid introduction of new coins without the difficulty, expense, and inconvenience of modifying existing coin rejectors. On the other hand, the clad coins would be more expensive to produce than the straight cupronickel alloy and strip will have to be purchased from outside suppliers.

Public Acceptability

These cupronickel clad coins would be only slightly lighter in weight than the existing coinage. The color of the coins with cupronickel cladding is very good. Because of the copper core, a reddened edge is exposed in the blanking process. Milling of the coins improves their appearance. Wear tests conducted by Battelle and by the Mint technical staff point to an expected average life of 20 to 30 years....

Operation in Vending Machines

As recommended by Battelle, the Mint and the rejector industry have conducted extensive testing of the operation of cupronickel clad coins in existing vending machines. This testing has demonstrated that when produced according to specifications (which are not intolerably narrow) these coins work in unaltered vending machine rejectors.

Counterfeiting Potential

The reddened edge of these coins and the difficult production process for the clad material from which they are made should insure against counterfeiting on any substantial scale....

Ease and Certainty of Production

The Mint has made sizable production runs using the cupronickel clad material and has not encountered any difficulties of consequence....

Cost and Availability of Raw Materials

The availability of the cupronickel clad strip from outside suppliers has been under intensive investigation by the Mint. This investigation is continuing but enough is known at this time to insure that adequate supplies of the strip will be available to support the full-scale production effort on the new coins that will be necessary during any transition to a new coinage system....

Conclusion: Acceptable coinage material.

Titanium

Titanium has been suggested to the Treasury as a coinage material but does not appear to be suitable. A major shortcoming is the alloy's light weight. No work is known to have been done on the rejector problem, nor is there any experience with mint fabrication of the metal. The melting point of titanium is too high to permit the use of ordinary brass mill equipment.

Conclusion: Rejected.

Zirconium-Hafnium

Zirconium-hafnium has been suggested to the Treasury as a possible alloy from which 50-cent pieces might be made. However, the cost of the alloy would appear to be prohibitive, wholly aside from other considerations. Zirconium strip was quoted to the Treasury at about $8 per pound—the 1963 *Minerals Yearbook* quotes $10 to $14 per pound. However, the addition of hafnium, recommended to enable the detection of counterfeit coins, would raise the price sharply. Hafnium is quoted at $138 a pound. One company thought that a zirconium 88-hafnium 12 alloy could be provided at a cost about equal to silver with some chance that the resulting volume of production might lower the cost to 50 percent of silver. Under the circumstances, neither zirconium nor zirconium-hafnium appears to be eligible coin alloy.

Conclusion: Rejected....

The text of this book is set in Times Roman, a face designed in 1931-2 for *The Times* of London by the British typographer and type designer Stanley Morrison. Originally cut for the Monotype, it was adapted to the Linotype in 1935 and has, since World War II, become one of the most popular type faces for book and publication printing.

The chapter headings and running headlines are set in the bold weight of Futura, the now classic 20th Century sans serif face designed in 1927 by Paul Renner for the Bauer Type Foundry of Frankfurt a/M., Germany, and now used—with and without acknowledgment and/or permission—throughout the Western world.